Good Housekeeping
COOKING FOR
vegetarian
CHILDREN

Janet Smith and Fiona Hunter

EBURY PRESS
LONDON

First published 1994

1 3 5 7 9 10 8 6 4 2

Text copyright © Janet Smith, Fiona Hunter and
The National Magazine Company Ltd 1994

Photography copyright © Ebury Press 1994

First published in the United Kingdom in 1994 by Ebury Press,
Random House, 20 Vauxhall Bridge Road, London SW1V 2SA

Random House Australia (Pty) Limited
20 Alfred Street, Milsons Point, Sydney,
New South Wales 2061, Australia

Random House New Zealand Limited
18 Poland Road, Glenfield,
Auckland 10, New Zealand

Random House South Africa (Pty) Limited
PO Box 337, Bergvlei, South Africa

Random House UK Limited Reg. No. 954009

A CIP catalogue record for this book is available from the British
Library.

Photography: James Murphy

Editor: Helen Southall
Design: Janet James

ISBN 0 09 178433 6

Typeset by Textype Typesetters, Cambridge
Printed by Tien Wah Press, Singapore

CONTENTS

INTRODUCTION

Vegetarianism is not a new concept, but what *is* a fairly recent phenomenon is the growing number of people who choose to adopt a vegetarian diet. In the last 10 years, the number of vegetarians in Britain has doubled; it is estimated that 7 per cent of the population (over 3 million people) are now vegetarian and it is among the younger age groups that this trend is growing fastest. One in six young people under the age of 16 do not eat meat.

People choose to become vegetarian for a variety of reasons. For many vegetarians, particularly children and young people, animal welfare is the most common reason. The slaughter of animals for food, and the cruelty and suffering inflicted upon animals reared for food, are considered unnecessary and immoral. For older children, the effect of meat production on the environment, such as the destruction of vast areas of rain forest for cattle ranching, can be the reason. Others consider it a waste of resources to use land to raise animals for food when using the same land to grow crops would be a more efficient way of producing food.

Whatever reason your children give for becoming vegetarian, it is important to respect their wishes and not to dismiss it as a 'fad'. Encourage them to learn more about the subject and the importance of choosing a healthy vegetarian diet.

What is a vegetarian diet?

The term 'vegetarianism' covers a broad spectrum of diets, with varying degrees of restriction. By definition, all vegetarians aim to exclude meat and fish from their diets as well as products derived from the slaughter of animals, such as gelatine, suet and lard. Depending on their commitment, vegetarians may also choose not to eat any eggs from battery farmed hens, or cheese made with rennet. In practice, however, many people call themselves 'vegetarian', yet excluding meat is the only concession they make.

Vegans, sometimes called 'strict vegetarians', avoid all animal products, including foods such as honey. **Lacto-ovo-vegetarians** avoid meat and fish but will eat dairy products and eggs (usually only free-range).

More extreme forms of vegetarian diet do exist but they are not widely practised: As well as avoiding meat and fish, **fruitarians** do not eat vegetables, though they will eat fruits, nuts and seeds. Their diet is based on a belief that it is wrong to kill plants by eating their roots, leaves, buds or stems. This is obviously a very restrictive diet and one which is not suitable for children as it cannot provide all the nutrients a growing child needs. A **macrobiotic** diet is followed for spiritual and philosophical reasons. Based on Chinese philosophy, it aims to maintain a balance between yin (positive) and yang (negative) foods. The diet progresses through 10 levels, becoming increasingly restrictive. Not all levels are vegetarian, though each level gradually eliminates animal products. The advanced stages of the diet are very restrictive and therefore not suitable for children and adolescents.

Common questions asked about a vegetarian diet

Can it provide all the nutrients necessary for a growing child?

This question causes concern for many parents with vegetarian children. The short answer is yes. In fact, a number of studies have shown that vegetarians are generally healthier than people who eat meat. However, a vegetarian diet does need to be well planned if it is to meet the increased nutritional demands of a growing child. There are some areas of nutrition that require special attention for *all* vegetarians, and these are particularly important for children because their needs are higher than those of adults.

Will it mean extra shopping and cooking?

Fortunately, being vegetarian these days doesn't mean you have to trail around health food shops in search of exotic and expensive ingredients. Nor do you need to spend hours in the kitchen making such things as nut roast and lentil casserole! Most supermarkets now stock everything you need, and vegetarian meals can be quick and easy to prepare. There are also growing numbers of ready-made vegetarian meals available, along with a wide range of convenience foods. Look out for the vegetarian symbol when shopping. Products approved by the Vegetarian Society will carry the Society's logo, guaranteeing that all the ingredients in those products have been scrutinised, but many supermarket chains have devised their own system for labelling suitable products. Alternatively, write to your local supermarket and ask for a list of the products they sell that are suitable for vegetarians and vegans.

Is a vegetarian diet more expensive?

A vegetarian diet should be no more expensive than one that includes meat. In fact, it should be cheaper. Choose fruit and vegetables when they are in season and at their cheapest. Dried beans and pulses are more economical than canned, but it's tempting to use canned to avoid the lengthy preparation of dried beans. If you have a freezer, however, dried beans can be soaked and cooked in bulk, and then frozen until needed.

What about school meals?

Fortunately, the majority of schools these days provide vegetarian meals, although parents may need to write to schools to request vegetarian meals on behalf of their children. In the unlikely event of a school not offering a vegetarian choice, a packed lunch is the only answer (see pages 44-54).

How do you cope when only one member of the family is vegetarian?

Obviously you can't expect the whole family to adopt a vegetarian diet just because one member has chosen that way of eating, but it's not unreasonable to expect the rest of the family to eat vegetarian meals once or twice a week. Rather than preparing different meals, adapt them to make them suitable for both groups. A casserole, for instance, can be made with beans and vegetables in one pan while the meat is cooked separately and just given to the meat-eaters. Many family favourites, such as lasagne or shepherd's pie, can be adapted to make them vegetarian by using textured vegetable protein (TVP) or Quorn (see page 11) instead of meat.

The nutritional needs of vegetarian children

Protein P

Protein has many important functions in the body. It is essential for the growth and repair of body tissues and therefore particularly important for growing children. Proteins are made up of amino acids. There are 20 amino acids in total, and nine of these are essential for children (eight for adults) – 'essential' because they cannot be made by the body and therefore must be provided by the diet. Unlike animal proteins, individual plant proteins do not contain all the essential amino acids in the necessary proportions. However, when different plant proteins are eaten together, they will complement each other and provide the body with all the amino acids it needs. In the past, vegetarians have been advised to combine different plant sources of protein within the same meal to ensure a good supply of all the essential amino acids. It is now known that this is not necessary providing a range of protein foods is eaten over the course of one day.

Good vegetarian sources of protein: **dairy products** (milk, cheese, yogurt, fromage frais); **eggs**; **nuts** (hazel, brazil, almonds, cashew, walnuts, pine kernels, chestnuts, pistachio); **seeds** (sesame, pumpkin, sunflower); **grains** (wheat in bread, flour and pasta, etc., barley, rye, oats, millet, maize (sweetcorn), rice, breakfast cereals); **soya products** (tofu, tempeh, textured vegetable protein, soya milk); **pulses** (peas, beans, lentils, peanuts).

NB Whole nuts should never be given to children under the age of five because of the risk of choking. They can be used in cooking if very finely chopped or ground.

Energy

Vegetarian diets, particularly those that contain very few or no animal products, are usually lower in fat and higher in fibre than diets that include meat. As a result, they also contain fewer calories. Although this is exactly the sort of diet recommended for most adults, it can present problems for young children because low-fat, high-fibre diets are less energy-dense. High-fibre meals can be very bulky, and sometimes it is difficult for young children, with small appetites and stomachs, to eat enough food to meet their energy requirements. For this reason, low-fat dairy products, such as skimmed milk, are not recommended for the under-fives. To ensure that energy needs are met, include energy-dense foods such as cheese, yogurt, full-fat milk, avocado, pulses (with a little vegetable oil added for extra energy), nuts and seeds in the diet.

Iron I

Iron is essential for the formation of red blood cells. Although it is present in many vegetarian foods, iron from plant sources is not as easily absorbed by the body as that from animal sources. Moreover, high intakes of dietary fibre and phytate (a substance found in whole grains) can interfere with the absorption of iron by binding to it and making it unavailable to the body. Absorption of iron is enhanced if vitamin C is eaten at the same meal. Citrus fruits and vegetables are both good sources of vitamin C. If your children won't eat vegetables, encourage them to drink fruit juice with their meals. (Fruit juice should be diluted for the under-fives.) Dairy products are a poor source of iron, so make sure your child doesn't have an over-dependency on these foods.

There is some evidence to suggest that people who have been following a vegetarian diet for some time adapt to lower intakes of iron by becoming more efficient at absorbing it. Nevertheless, new vegetarians (particularly menstruating girls and women who are more vulnerable to anaemia because of their monthly blood loss) may benefit from taking an iron supplement. Iron is toxic in large doses and supplements can cause digestive upsets, so always follow manufacturers' recommendations and keep supplements out of the reach of young children.

Good vegetarian sources of iron: **cereals**; **dark green leafy vegetables** (spinach, cabbage, watercress); **dried fruit**; **wholemeal bread**; **nuts**; **beans** and **pulses**.

Zinc Z

This essential mineral is involved in a number of body processes, including growth. It is often found in lower amounts in vegetarian and vegan diets and, like iron, its absorption can be reduced by the presence of phytate and dietary fibre.

Good vegetarian sources of zinc: **yeast**; **nuts**; **dairy products**; **whole grain cereals**; **tahini** (see page 33); **beans** and **pulses**. **Pumpkin seeds** provide one of the most concentrated vegetarian sources of zinc.

Vitamin B$_{12}$ VB$_{12}$

This vitamin is needed by the body in minute amounts for growth and the formation of red blood cells. It is also important in helping to maintain a healthy nervous system. Vitamin B$_{12}$ is found in animal products, so vegetarians eating dairy products or eggs are likely to get enough, but vegans need to make sure they supplement their diet in some way. A number of foods, for example yeast extract, breakfast cereals, margarines and soya milk, are fortified with B$_{12}$; one easy way to ensure a regular intake of B$_{12}$ is always to use fortified yeast extract when making soups, gravies, casseroles, etc. Only a small amount of B$_{12}$ can be absorbed at any one time so high-dose supplements are not recommended unless prescribed by your doctor.

Good vegetarian sources of vitamin B$_{12}$: **dairy products**; **eggs**; **fortified products** (breakfast cereals, yeast extract, soya milk, TVP).

Vitamin D VD

Vitamin D is essential for growth, the absorption of calcium and the formation of strong bones and teeth. It is found naturally only in a very few foods, all of which are of animal origin. However, it is also made by human skin when it is exposed to sunlight. Vegetarians who are confined indoors, or who have religious beliefs that involve covering up most of the skin, should make sure they include fortified foods, such as soya milk and/or margarine, in their diet, or they should take a vitamin D supplement.

Children have an increased requirement for vitamin D because of their growing bones; they may need a supplement, especially in the winter months. The vitamin is available in a number of different forms – D$_3$ may be of animal origin so strict vegetarians should take D$_2$.

Good vegetarian sources of vitamin D: **egg yolks**; **milk**. All margarines, breakfast cereals and soya milk are fortified with vitamin D.

Riboflavin VB_2

Vitamin B_2, or riboflavin, is essential for the release of energy from food. Dairy products are a good source of riboflavin but cereals are relatively lacking.

Good vegan sources of riboflavin: **yeast extract**; **almonds**; **green vegetables** and **pulses**.

Calcium C

Essential for the formation of strong bones and teeth, calcium is therefore of great importance to children and young people. (Although our bones stop growing in length at around 18 years of age, they continue to get thicker until our mid-thirties.) Calcium absorption can be inhibited by the presence of phytic acid in bran and whole grain cereals, and by oxalic acid found in certain vegetables.

Good vegetarian sources of calcium: **milk**; **yogurt**; **cheese**; **eggs**; **sesame seeds** and **tahini** (see page 33); **almonds**; **brazil nuts**; **tofu**; **dried fruit**; **fortified soya milk**; **green leafy vegetables**; **pulses**. Calcium is more easily absorbed from dairy products than from other sources.

SUGGESTED DAILY EATING PLAN FOR VEGETARIAN CHILDREN

This should only be used as a rough guide; a 'serving' refers to an average-sized children's portion.

• **grains, breakfast cereals, bread, pasta, rice, buckwheat, millet, bulgar wheat, potatoes** – four or five servings a day or more to satisfy appetite
• **fruit and vegetables** – five or more servings a day
• **pulses, nuts or seeds** – two or three servings a day
• **milk, yogurt, cheese, eggs, soya products** – two or three servings a day
• **fat (butter, margarine, oil)** – in moderate amounts
• **sugar** – not necessary in diet but can be eaten in moderate amounts
• a product such as yeast extract which is fortified with vitamin B_{12}

Feeding vegetarian children

It is important to establish healthy eating habits early in life, so they become second nature to children as they grow up. The key to a balanced diet, whether vegetarian or otherwise, is to eat a variety of foods. Children should be offered foods they can enjoy and cope with, and they should not be forced to eat anything they are determined not to. Faddy eating habits are often a problem as children get older and a bit more independent; thankfully it's usually only a passing phase.

Young children need frequent between-meals snacks in order to obtain sufficient energy. Try to avoid giving too many sweets, shop-bought cakes or biscuits, sweetened fizzy drinks or salty snacks. Instead, offer sandwiches, fruit, scones, malt bread or homemade cakes or biscuits (see pages 104–119 for ideas).

Children naturally like the taste of sugar and sweet foods. Whilst it's not practical or necessary to avoid sugar altogether, it is a major factor contributing to tooth decay so it should only be allowed in moderation.

Vegetarian teenagers

It is amongst this age group that the number of new converts to vegetarianism is growing fastest. According to a recent survey, 11 per cent of girls aged between 13 and 15 are vegetarian.

It can be tempting for parents to dismiss this as a fad or passing phase and, while this may sometimes be the case, it is important that parents respect their children's decision. Encourage them to learn more about vegetarianism and the importance of choosing a balanced diet. The Vegetarian Society produces a range of leaflets aimed at this age group (send a stamped, addressed envelope to the Vegetarian Society, Parkdale, Dunham Road, Altrincham, Cheshire WA14 4QG, or telephone 061–928 0793).

The teenage years are another period of rapid growth, and this is usually accompanied, especially in boys, by what can seem an endless appetite. Encourage them to fill up on starchy foods, such as wholemeal bread, pasta or rice. Breakfast cereals are an ideal snack food at any time of the day.

Many girls, and a growing number of boys, in this age group are concerned about their weight. Unfortunately, it's easy for slimming to get out of control. Parents should keep this in mind, and at the first sign of any eating disorder contact their GP or one of the eating disorder associations. While a vegetarian diet is perfectly capable of providing the nutritional needs of a teenager, the combination of a vegetarian diet with the restricted food intake that occurs when slimming can make a vitamin supplement a good idea. Choose a multivitamin and mineral supplement. Supplements are also a good idea for fussy eaters and teenage girls with heavy periods.

Fiona Hunter

UNDERSTANDING THE NUTRITIONAL SYMBOLS

All the recipes in this book have been carefully planned with the needs of vegetarian children in mind, and will help towards providing a varied, balanced diet. Some recipes, however, are a particularly good source of important nutrients, as indicated by the following symbols.

P	Protein	**VA**	Vitamin A
I	Iron	**VB$_2$**	Vitamin B$_2$ (riboflavin)
C	Calcium	**VB$_{12}$**	Vitamin B$_{12}$
F	Fibre	**VC**	Vitamin C
FA	Folic Acid	**VD**	Vitamin D
		VE	Vitamin E

For more information on the nutrients that are particularly important for vegetarian children, see pages 6–8.

A word about ingredients

Eggs

Most vegetarians choose to eat free-range eggs because they consider battery farming inhumane. When looking for free-range eggs, don't be misled by a picture of chickens in a farmyard setting on the box; unless it says they are free-range they are from battery hens.

The wholesome, good-for-you image of the egg has been tarnished by the slight risk of salmonella bacteria being present in eggs. As a parent, it's hard to know what to do for the best. Firstly, make sure the eggs you use are fresh. Always check the sell- and use-by dates; a fresh egg will sink in a bowl of cold water and a stale egg will float. Store eggs in the refrigerator, not in a warm kitchen. Give only hard-boiled eggs to very young children and babies, but for older children half the pleasure of eating a boiled egg is removed if the yolk is too hard to dip 'soldiers' into. Aim to boil eggs until the white is completely set and the yolk just soft.

Buying egg-containing products like mayonnaise from a health food shop means that the eggs used to make them are more likely to be free-range, but you should always check the label, nevertheless. Look out, too, for vegan, egg-free mayonnaise, or see the recipe on page 122.

Cheese

Don't forget that cheese is not always completely vegetarian; many types contain animal rennet. Some vegetarians will eat this but many insist on a completely vegetarian cheese. Most supermarkets and delicatessens now stock a wide range of these. Many familiar brands of soft or cream cheeses are vegetarian and always have been.

Vegetarian versions of cheeses such as Parmesan are available, but can be harder to track down. If you do have problems, it's worth contacting the Vegetarian Society (address on page 9), who publish a comprehensive list of suppliers.

Soya cheese is the vegan option. It's fine in sauces and as a topping, but in something uncooked, like a sandwich, it's not much of a substitute for the real thing.

Margarine

Not all brands of margarine are entirely vegetarian as some are manufactured from fish oils and rennet containing whey, so it is important to read labels carefully. Solid vegetable margarine for pastry-making, and vegetable suet are now widely available, too.

Tofu

Tofu is an incredibly versatile product. It is made from a compressed paste of soya beans, so it is very high in protein, low in fat and easy to digest. It is virtually tasteless so if puréed and mixed into soups and sauces, picky eaters will not notice it is there. For puréeing, soft, silken tofu is the best choice, but firm tofu can be sliced or cut into chunks and included in curries and casseroles, or try it coated with breadcrumbs and fried. To add flavour, marinate beforehand in a strongly flavoured mixture (perhaps containing onion or spring onion). Smoked tofu has a subtle smoky flavour and can be used as it is; try it on baked potatoes or pizzas.

Once removed from the packet, any leftover tofu must be stored in a bowl of cold water in the refrigerator. Change the water daily and it should keep for a week.

TVP (Textured Vegetable Protein)

TVP is another soya product. It is manufactured specifically to resemble meat – either mince or chunks. Unlike tofu, it has some flavour and a chewy, slightly meat-like texture. This puts some vegetarians off, but for new converts to vegetarianism it has some appeal. Its other advantage is that it allows those who find themselves cooking for vegetarians for the first time to cook their repertoire of meat-based recipes – bolognese, shepherd's pie, lasagne, chilli, and the like – in a vegetarian form. This can be useful until you get to know some new recipes!

Most TVP is sold as a dehydrated product so it needs soaking beforehand, and it takes longer to cook than meat mince. However, frozen TVP mince, which can be used straight from the freezer, has just come on to the market and is very good. Look out for it in health food shops.

Quorn

Quorn is another 'meat substitute'. It is low in fat and calories, yet high in protein and fibre. It is not suitable for vegans, and some vegetarians prefer to avoid it because it contains egg albumen from battery hens.

Gelatine

Mousses and jellies set with gelatine are out of the question for vegetarians, since gelatine is produced from boiled beef bones. The alternatives are agar-agar and Gelozone. Unfortunately, because neither product reacts in quite the same way as gelatine, they are not completely interchangeable in recipes. Both products are available from health food shops. Agar-agar is a tasteless white powder derived from seaweed. Unlike gelatine, it will only dissolve when it is boiled. Allow about 10ml (2 tsp) per 600ml (1 pint) of liquid.

Gelozone is also a tasteless white powder made from vegetable ingredients. Dissolve it in cold water, then heat until the liquid is steaming but not boiling. Allow about 7ml (1 *heaped* tsp) to each 600ml (1 pint) liquid. If setting something acidic, however, you will need to use double this amount.

Milk

Choose soya milk for vegans; it's now available sweetened, unsweetened and fortified with calcium. Green top (unpasteurised) milk, sheep's milk and goats' milk are all unsuitable for children under the age of 5 years.

Flour – wholemeal versus white

Where it makes a difference to the finished result of the recipes in this book, we have specified one or the other type of flour, but generally speaking, the choice is yours. Children tend to prefer the lighter texture of cakes, pastries and breads made with white flour or a 50/50 mixture of white and wholemeal. Don't try to give your children too much fibre. It's unnecessary and the bulk of these foods means that they feel full before they have eaten enough to provide them with the other nutrients they need.

Pulses

The term 'pulse' covers all the various beans, peas and lentils that have been preserved by drying. Pulses are an important source of protein, carbohydrate and fibre in a vegetarian diet. Most also contain significant amounts of iron, potassium, calcium, and some B vitamins. Soya beans are unique in that they contain complete protein (see page 6) as well as more calcium and iron than other pulses.

Store pulses in airtight containers in a cool, dark place. They keep well, but after about 6 months their skins begin to toughen and they take increasingly longer to cook, so buy them from a supplier with a fast turnover of stock.

Before cooking, all beans (with the exception of lentils and split peas) should be soaked overnight in a large bowl of cold water. In the morning, drain them, bring to the boil in fresh water and boil rapidly for 10 minutes (to destroy the toxins present in some beans – although it is not strictly necessary for all beans it does them no harm and saves the problem of remembering which types require fast boiling), then simmer until the beans are tender (see chart opposite). Add salt about 15 minutes before the end of the cooking time; salt added at the beginning of cooking tends to toughen the skins. The flavour can be subtly enhanced by the addition of a couple of bay leaves or cloves of garlic, or a peeled onion studded with a few cloves, to the cooking water.

To save time, there is a quick-soak method that works just as well. Put the beans into a saucepan, cover with cold water and bring to the boil. Boil rapidly for 10 minutes, then remove from the heat. Cover the pan and leave the beans to soak in the same water for 3 hours. Drain and cook in fresh water for the usual time (see chart).

Although canned beans often have sugar and salt added, they're a good quick alternative to cooking your own. It's a good idea to empty them from the can straight into a colander or sieve and rinse them under cold running water before use. They tend to be quite soft, so add them to chilli, casseroles, stews and curries towards the end of the cooking time.

A 425g (15oz) can of beans, drained, is roughly equivalent to 225g (8oz) cooked beans, or 125g (4oz) dried (uncooked) beans. The weight of dried pulses approximately doubles during cooking, so if a recipe calls for 225g (8oz) cooked beans you will need 125g (4oz) to start with. Drained, cooked pulses will keep for several days in a covered container in the refrigerator. Alternatively, freeze them in usable quantities. Thaw overnight and use as freshly cooked beans.

To cook pulses in a pressure cooker
To cut down on lengthy cooking times, pulses can be pressure cooked (see chart for times). Overnight soaking is not necessary – just cover with boiling water and leave to soak for 1 hour. Drain, then transfer to the pressure cooker with 600ml (1 pint) water for every 225g (8oz) beans (weighed after soaking). The cooker must not be more than one-third full.

Bring to the boil, then remove any skum that has risen to the surface. Lower the heat so that the beans are simmering gently, then put the lid on the pan. Bring up to pressure and cook for the time given in the chart. Reduce the pressure slowly. Season with salt while warm.

Do not cook mixtures of different types of pulses in the pressure cooker at the same time. This is potentially dangerous as over-cooked beans can rise up in the pan and block the safety valves and air vents.

COOKING PULSES

TYPE	COOKING TIME AFTER SOAKING	PRESSURE COOKING TIME High (15 lb) pressure
Aduki beans	30–60 minutes	12 minutes
Black beans	1½ hours	20 minutes
Black-eyed beans	1½ hours	12 minutes
Butter beans	1½ hours	17 minutes
Cannellini beans	1 hour	25 minutes
Chick peas	1½–2 hours	20 minutes
Flageolet beans	1 hour	15 minutes
Haricot beans	1–1½ hours	20 minutes
Lentils (green)	30 minutes	15 minutes
Lentils (split red) (no need to soak)	15–25 minutes	not recommended
Mung beans	40 minutes	12 minutes
Red kidney beans	1–1½ hours	20 minutes
Rose cocoa or borlotti beans	1 hour	17 minutes
Soya beans	3–4 hours	30 minutes
Split peas	45–60 minutes	15 minutes

The cooking times given above are approximate and depend on the age of the beans and the soaking time.

BREAKFASTS

Breakfast fruit salad

Dried apricots contain significant amounts of vitamins and minerals, including iron; they also add a good 'bite' to fruit salads. Serve this salad on its own or topped with natural or fruit yogurt, or sprinkle with a little Crunchy breakfast cereal (see page 17).

Serves 4

75g (3oz) no-need-to-soak dried apricots, chopped	1 large slice of watermelon or melon of your choice (about 175g/6oz)
300ml (½ pint) pineapple, apple or orange juice	1 banana
2 large juicy oranges	
about 125g (4oz) strawberries or seedless grapes	

1 Mix the apricots with the fruit juice in a large bowl and leave to soak while you prepare the other fruits. Peel and segment the oranges, and cut each segment in half if large. Halve the strawberries and any large grapes, if using. Remove the seeds and skin from the watermelon and cut the flesh into bite-sized cubes. Stir all the fruit into the apricot and juice mixture.

2 Just before serving, peel and slice the banana and add to the rest of the fruit. Stir gently to mix.

NUTRITION

Good source of

F   **VA**   **VC**

Breakfast fruit salad (above), Crunchy breakfast cereal (page 17), Yogurt (page 16)

Yogurt

Yogurt is easy and cheap to make at home, and children find the process fascinating.
Use full-fat milk and skimmed milk powder to make a smooth,
creamy yogurt. To make fruit yogurt, add about 150ml (¼ pint) sweetened fruit purée
to the finished yogurt.

Makes about 600ml (1 pint)

600ml (1 pint) full-fat pasteurised or UHT milk	**15ml (1 tbsp) 'live' natural yogurt**
30ml (2 level tbsp) skimmed milk powder	

1 Bring the milk and skimmed milk powder to the boil in a large, heavy-based saucepan. Remove from the heat and leave to cool to 43°C (110°F). (You will need a thermometer to check the temperature.) If using UHT milk it does not have to be boiled; just heated to the correct temperature.

2 Meanwhile, rinse a clean wide-necked vacuum flask or a 900ml (1½ pint) container (with a lid) with boiling water.

3 When the milk is the correct temperature, gradually blend it into the yogurt. Pour into the warmed vacuum flask or container, replace the lid and leave in a warm place for 6–8 hours, undisturbed, until just set. (Once you've made your own yogurt a few times you will get to know how long it takes.)

4 As soon as it it set, transfer the yogurt to the refrigerator to chill. Once set, yogurt is best used within 4 days. Save some of the yogurt for making your next batch.

NUTRITION

Good source of

C

NOTES

You can make vegan yogurt with soya milk, but the first batch will not be totally vegan because of the spoonful of 'starter' yogurt used. However, if you use a spoonful of your first batch to make a second, then that will be almost totally vegan.

If the yogurt does not set it could be because the milk was not brought up to boiling point; the milk was stale to start with; the 'starter' yogurt was not mixed in properly; the 'starter' was not 'live'; the temperature was not correct – too high when the 'starter' was added or not warm enough when the finished yogurt was left to set. Too much 'starter' makes sour, grainy yogurt.

Crunchy breakfast cereal

You can adapt this recipe to suit your children. If they don't like sultanas or raisins, use chopped dried apricots or dried apple instead. The flaked almonds could be replaced with peanuts, brazil nuts or walnuts. Serve the cereal plain or with fruit, yogurt or milk. It can also be munched just as it comes as a snack.

Serves 6

150ml (¼ pint) pineapple or apple juice	25g (1oz) sunflower seeds
45ml (3 tbsp) runny honey	50g (2oz) flaked almonds
125g (4oz) jumbo oats	50g (2oz) sultanas or raisins
25g (1oz) sesame seeds	

1 Put the fruit juice in a bowl and stir in the honey. Pour over the oats, stir and leave to soak overnight. The next morning, all the liquid will have been absorbed by the oats. Add the sesame seeds, sunflower seeds and almonds, and mix thoroughly.

2 Spread the mixture in a thin layer on one or two greased non-stick baking sheets. Bake in the oven at 200°C (400°F) mark 6 for about 30 minutes or until golden brown and crunchy. Stir the mixture occasionally as it cooks so that it browns evenly.

3 Break the cereal up into small pieces and mix with the sultanas or raisins. Leave to cool completely, then store in an airtight container, where it will keep for up to 2 weeks.

VARIATION

Banana and Coconut Crunch Replace the sunflower seeds with banana chips. In step 2, sprinkle the mixture with 40g (1½oz) desiccated coconut after it has been cooking for about 20 minutes. Return to the oven for another 10 minutes.

Potato cakes

I doubt if you'll have time to make these very often, but they are good for late weekend breakfasts. I've tried making them with leftover boiled potatoes – they work quite well providing you have a waxy variety (so they don't turn into a mush). Alternatively, you could cook the potatoes in advance to save time in the morning, or you could cook the potato cakes in advance and simply reheat them in a hot oven for about 10 minutes. Serve with poached eggs or grilled tomatoes and lettuce.

Makes 6

2 medium potatoes (about 350g/12oz total weight)	salt and pepper
125g (4oz) low-fat soft cheese	vegetable oil for frying
2 spring onions, trimmed and finely chopped	

1 Parboil the potatoes in their skins for about 8 minutes, or until they begin to feel soft. Drain, rinse in cold water to cool them quickly, then leave them until they are cool enough to handle.

2 Finely grate the potatoes into a bowl and add the cheese and spring onions. Season with salt and pepper, and mix well. Divide the mixture into 6 equal portions.

3 Heat a little oil in a large, non-stick frying pan. Add one portion of the potato mixture and quickly pat it out in the frying pan using the back of a wooden spoon until it is quite thin and measures about 12.5cm (5 inches) in diameter. Cook over a high heat until golden brown on the underside, then turn over and cook the second side. Check that the potato is cooked in the centre. Remove from the pan, drain on absorbent kitchen paper and keep warm while cooking the remaining potato cakes. Serve hot.

Sweet pancakes

Whether eaten plain, with a squeeze of lemon juice and a light sprinkling of sugar, or more elaborately with maple syrup and banana, pancakes for breakfast are a delicious treat and the fun of making and cooking them should tempt the most unenthusiastic of eaters. Omit the almonds if making the pancakes for very young children.

Makes about 8

125g (4oz) plain white flour	finely grated rind of 1 lemon or 1 small orange
a pinch of salt	vegetable oil for cooking
30ml (2 level tbsp) icing sugar	a few toasted flaked almonds (optional)
1 free-range egg	
about 300ml (½ pint) milk	

1 Sift the flour, salt and sugar into a bowl and make a well in the centre. Add the egg, pour in half the milk and beat together in the well, gradually beating in the flour from the sides of the well until you have a very thick batter. Slowly pour in enough of the remaining milk, beating all the time, until the batter has the consistency of single cream. Add the grated lemon or orange rind. (Alternatively, to mix the batter in a food processor, put the milk and egg in first, process to mix, then add the dry ingredients. Process for a few more seconds until smooth.)

2 Heat a little oil in a 15cm (6 inch) frying pan until hot. Swirl it round so that it coats the base and sides of the pan, then pour off any excess. Pour in about 45ml (3 tbsp) of the batter, or enough to coat the base of the pan thinly. Sprinkle with a few almonds, if using, then cook until the pancake is golden brown on the underside.

3 Turn or toss the pancake and cook the second side until golden brown. Remove from the pan and cook the remaining pancakes in the same way, adding more oil to the pan as necessary. As each pancake is cooked, either serve immediately, or pile them up, interleaved with greaseproof paper, and keep them warm in the oven until they are all cooked.

Pear and oat pancakes

These are quite quick to cook in the morning, or they can be made in advance and frozen. To serve, arrange frozen pancakes on a baking sheet, cover and reheat in the oven at 180°C (350°F) mark 4 for about 15 minutes. Serve the warm pancakes topped with a few slices of fruit and a spoonful of natural yogurt or fromage frais.

Makes about 14

1 free-range egg	2.5ml (½ level tsp) salt
300ml (½ pint) milk	1 pear
25g (1oz) vegetable margarine or butter, melted	50g (2oz) dried stoned dates, chopped, or raisins
50g (2oz) plain wholemeal flour	vegetable oil for cooking
50g (2oz) porridge oats	

1 Whisk together the egg, milk and melted margarine or butter. Add the flour, oats and salt, and whisk again until thoroughly mixed. Cover and leave to stand for at least 30 minutes or overnight.

2 Peel, core and grate the pear, and fold it into the pancake mixture with the dates or raisins.

3 Heat a little oil in a heavy-based, non-stick frying pan. Put about 30ml (2 tbsp) pancake mixture into the pan. Add more mixture to the pan, 30ml (2 tbsp) at a time, to make more pancakes, until the pan is full. Make sure that you leave plenty of space between them. Cook until bubbles appear on the surface and the underside of each pancake is golden brown.

4 Turn the pancakes over and cook until the second side is golden brown. Remove from the pan, cover and keep warm while cooking the remainder. Serve warm.

Muffins

If you haven't got a proper muffin tin, you could make these in paper bun cases on a baking sheet. Use two paper cases for each muffin.

Makes about 12

50g (2oz) vegetable margarine or butter	125g (4oz) self-raising wholemeal flour
200ml (7 fl oz) milk	225g (8oz) sultanas, raspberries, blackcurrants, blueberries or chocolate chips
1 free-range egg	
175g (6oz) soft brown sugar	
a pinch of salt	
225g (8oz) self-raising white flour	

1 Line 12 deep muffin tins with paper cases. Melt the margarine or butter, add all the remaining ingredients, except the fruit or chocolate chips, and mix thoroughly to make a smooth batter. Fold in the fruit or chocolate chips.

2 Spoon the mixture into the paper cases and bake in the oven at 220°C (425°F) mark 7 for about 20 minutes or until well risen and firm to the touch. Serve warm, fresh from the oven, or leave to cool on a wire rack and store in an airtight container.

Porridge with apple and sultanas

If you're serving this to adults as well as children, remove the children's portions first, then boost the fibre content of the remaining porridge by sprinkling it with a little bran. Cook it for a few more minutes before serving.

Serves 4

600ml (1 pint) water	1 eating apple, peeled, cored and chopped
75g (3oz) porridge oats	50g (2oz) sultanas
about 10ml (2 level tsp) sugar	

1 Pour the water into a non-stick saucepan and bring to the boil. Sprinkle in the oats and bring back to the boil, stirring.

2 Add the sugar, apple and sultanas to the porridge, lower the heat and simmer for 5 minutes or until thickened. Serve.

Muffins

Scrambled eggs with mushrooms

Try this as a change from boiled or poached eggs. The mushrooms could be replaced
with a few peas, a chopped tomato, a handful of sweetcorn or a finely
chopped red pepper. It's also nice with a little grated cheese stirred in towards the end
of cooking.

Serves 2–3

25g (1oz) vegetable margarine or butter	salt and pepper
125g (4oz) mushrooms, wiped and sliced	2–3 slices of wholemeal toast, to serve
4 free-range eggs, beaten	

1 Melt the margarine or butter in a non-stick saucepan. Add the mushrooms and cook over a fairly high heat until softened.
2 Add the eggs, lower the heat and cook, stirring all the time, until the eggs have just set. Season with a little salt and pepper. Serve piled on wholemeal toast.

NUTRITION

Good source of

P   VA   VB$_2$ VB$_{12}$

Dried fruit spread

Dried fruit is a concentrated source of iron, calcium and potassium, as well as vitamin A. Use this easy-to-make spread on toast instead of jams and preserves with a high sugar content. It will keep for up to 2 weeks in an airtight container in the refrigerator.

Makes about 450g (1lb)

75g (3oz) dried peaches, chopped	5ml (1 level tsp) grated orange rind
175g (6oz) dried stoned dates, chopped	1.25ml (¼ level tsp) ground cinnamon
175g (6oz) no-need-to-soak dried apricots, chopped	150ml (¼ pint) unsweetened orange juice
grated rind of ½ lemon	

1 Put all the ingredients into a saucepan. Bring to the boil, lower the heat and simmer very gently for 20 minutes or until the mixture is thick and the orange juice has evaporated. If the mixture shows signs of sticking, add a little extra fruit juice.

2 Mash with a fork until smooth, then put into washed and sterilised glass jars. Cover the spread with wax discs, waxed side down, and cover the jars with damp rounds of cellophane secured with rubber bands. Store in the refrigerator.

Breakfast shake

Filling, nutritious drinks like this make good breakfasts for fussy or lazy eaters, and for children who are feeling unwell. Sieve the drink after processing if your children don't like the bits in it.

Makes about 750ml (1¼ pints)

225g (8oz) ripe strawberries, raspberries or blackcurrants	**15–30ml (1–2 tbsp) runny honey**
1 small banana	**300ml (½ pint) chilled milk**
150g (5oz) carton of natural bio yogurt	**ice cubes, to serve**
10ml (2 tsp) lemon juice	

1 Hull or string the soft fruit, as necessary. Peel the banana and break into small pieces.
2 Put the fruit in a blender or food processor with all the remaining ingredients, except the ice, and process until smooth. Pour into tall glasses or beakers, add a few ice cubes and serve.

NUTRITION

Good source of

C   VA   VB₂   VC

SOUPS AND SNACKS

Carrot and parsnip soup

This creamy, mild, almost sweet-tasting soup should appeal to very young children.
Serve it barely warm; if toddlers have to wait for their food to cool, they can
be put off at the thought of it burning them, or they become bored and uninterested in
the whole idea of eating by the time it is ready. Serve the soup with crusty
French bread (without margarine or butter) to encourage chewing, or topped with
squares of cheese on toast sprinkled with sesame seeds. Similar to soured
cream, smetana is a good lower-fat substitute for single cream.

Serves 6–8

450g (1lb) carrots, peeled and sliced	1.1 litres (2 pints) vegetable stock
450g (1lb) parsnips, peeled and sliced	salt and pepper
1 large floury potato (such as King Edward or Maris Piper), peeled and roughly chopped	300ml (½ pint) creamed smetana
1 cooking apple, peeled, cored and chopped	

1 Put all the vegetables, the apple and stock in a large saucepan. Add salt and pepper to taste and bring to the boil, then reduce the heat and simmer for about 25 minutes or until everything is very tender. Leave to cool slightly, then purée in a blender or food processor.

2 Return the soup to the pan, add the smetana and reheat gently, stirring constantly, until warm.

NUTRITION

Good source of

VA   VC

Club sandwich (page 32), Carrot and parsnip soup (above)

Lentil and coconut soup

Coconut milk gives this soup a mild, creamy taste which most children love. For more sophisticated palates, you could fry a little grated fresh ginger with the onion and garlic.

Serves 6

15ml (1 tbsp) vegetable oil	60ml (4 tbsp) instant coconut milk powder
1 onion, skinned and chopped	1.1 litres (2 pints) vegetable stock
1 garlic clove, skinned and crushed (optional)	salt and pepper
2 carrots, peeled and finely chopped	toasted desiccated coconut, to serve
225g (8oz) split red lentils	

1 Heat the oil in a large saucepan, add the onion, garlic and carrots, and cook for a few minutes until the onion is beginning to soften, stirring all the time. Add the lentils and sprinkle in the coconut milk powder. Cook for a further 1–2 minutes, stirring all the time.

2 Add the stock and bring to the boil, then lower the heat and simmer gently for about 20 minutes or until the lentils are soft and mushy. Season with salt and pepper.

3 Leave the soup to cool slightly, then purée in a blender or food processor. Return to the pan and reheat. Serve hot, sprinkled with a little toasted coconut.

NUTRITION

Good source of

VA

Chunky vegetable and bean soup

This is my family's favourite soup. It's hearty and filling, and it's a great recipe for using up odds and ends of leftover vegetables. I always use canned beans for this because it tends to be a last-minute soup, but you could use dried beans you have cooked yourself, if you prefer (see page 12). If using canned beans, the recipe works well with most kinds, but aim to use two varieties of contrasting colour, shape and texture.

Serves 6–8

15ml (1 tbsp) olive oil	10ml (2 level tsp) mild curry paste
1 large onion, skinned and roughly chopped	about 1.4 litres (2½ pints) vegetable stock
2 garlic cloves, skinned and crushed	425g (15oz) can of red kidney beans, drained and rinsed
2 large parsnips, peeled and roughly chopped	425g (15oz) can of black-eyed beans, drained and rinsed
2 large carrots, peeled and thickly sliced	salt and pepper
2 large potatoes, peeled and roughly chopped	45ml (3 level tbsp) chopped fresh coriander
about 450g (1lb) of any other vegetables you have to hand, such as peppers, celery, turnips, leeks or more of the above	2 courgettes, trimmed and thinly sliced

1 Heat the oil in a large saucepan, add the onion, garlic, parsnips, carrots and potatoes, and cook over a high heat for a few minutes, stirring all the time. Add the mixed vegetables and the curry paste, and cook for a further 1–2 minutes. Add the stock, bring to the boil and simmer for about 25 minutes or until all the vegetables are tender.

2 Add the beans, and salt and pepper to taste. Leave the soup to cool slightly, then purée about half in a food processor. Return it to the pan, add the coriander and the courgettes and simmer for a further 10 minutes or until the courgettes are just tender. Serve hot.

NUTRITION

Good source of

F P I VA VB$_2$

Potato, leek and spinach soup

Soups are a good way to get children to eat green vegetables, and puréeing them with other vegetables means they almost go undetected! I find this soup is enjoyed more if a few pieces of potato are left whole.

Serves 6

450g (1lb) potatoes, peeled and cut into large chunks	225g (8oz) spinach, trimmed
	300ml (½ pint) milk
225g (8oz) trimmed leeks, roughly chopped	salt and pepper
600ml (1 pint) vegetable stock	freshly grated nutmeg, to taste

1 Put the potatoes, leeks and stock in a large saucepan, and bring to the boil. Lower the heat and simmer for about 25 minutes or until the vegetables are very soft.
2 Add the spinach and the milk and bring back to the boil. Remove some pieces of potato with a slotted spoon, then purée the soup in a blender or food processor. Return to the saucepan with the reserved potato and reheat. Season to taste with salt, pepper and nutmeg before serving hot.

NUTRITION

Good source of

VA **VC**

Creamy mushroom soup

Without altering the flavour of this soup, tofu increases its nutritional value as well as acting as a thickener and giving it a lovely creamy texture.

Serves 6

15ml (1 tbsp) vegetable oil	900ml (1½ pints) vegetable stock
1 onion, skinned and chopped	2 bay leaves
700g (1½lb) open-cup or field mushrooms, wiped and roughly chopped	300g (10½oz) silken tofu
	salt and pepper
1 large floury potato (such as King Edward or Maris Piper), peeled and finely diced	

1 Heat the oil in a large saucepan and cook the onion for about 5 minutes or until softened. Add the mushrooms and cook for a further 1 minute, stirring all the time. Add the potato, stock and bay leaves, and bring to the boil. Reduce the heat and simmer gently for 20 minutes or until the potato is just starting to break up. Leave to cool slightly.

2 Remove the bay leaves, then purée the soup in a blender or food processor with the tofu. Return the soup to the pan and heat gently until hot. Season with salt and pepper before serving.

NUTRITION

Good source of

C   VB$_2$ VC

Creamy tomato soup

In winter, when plump ripe tomatoes are not readily available, use canned tomatoes.

Serves 4–6

900g (2lb) very ripe tomatoes or two 400g (14oz) cans of chopped tomatoes	600ml (1 pint) vegetable stock
1 small onion, skinned and quartered	5ml (1 level tsp) sugar
1 garlic clove, skinned and crushed (optional)	225g (8oz) mascarpone or low- or medium-fat soft cheese
30ml (2 level tbsp) tomato purée	salt and pepper

1 Put the tomatoes, onion, garlic, if using, and tomato purée in a blender or food processor and process until very finely chopped. If you have used fresh tomatoes, push the mixture through a sieve to remove the skins.

2 Pour the chopped mixture into a saucepan, add the stock and sugar, and bring to the boil. Reduce the heat and simmer gently for 10 minutes, stirring occasionally. Add the soft cheese of your choice and continue to heat gently until the soup is hot and the cheese has melted. Season with salt and pepper, and serve hot.

NUTRITION

Good source of

VA   VC

Club sandwich

Grilling the red pepper makes it soft and more digestible. You can use homemade Creamy hummus (see page 33), or a shop-bought version, or you could replace the hummus with more mayonnaise, if preferred.

Makes 2 sandwiches

1 large red pepper	a few slices of cucumber
6 large thin slices of bread	60ml (4 tbsp) hummus
mayonnaise for spreading	salt and pepper
a few lettuce leaves	

1 Cut the pepper in half lengthways and remove the seeds and core. Cover the grill pan with a piece of foil (to save you having to wash it before making the toast) and lay the pepper halves on top, cut side down. Cook as close to the heat source as possible until the skin has blackened and blistered. Leave until cool enough to handle, then carefully peel off the skin.

2 Remove the foil from the grill pan and lightly toast the bread slices on both sides. Spread two slices with a little mayonnaise and top with lettuce leaves and cucumber. Spread two slices with hummus, top with the pepper halves, and season with a little salt and pepper. Put the pepper-topped slices on top of the lettuce-topped slices and top each with one of the remaining slices of toast. Cut each sandwich into four and serve immediately.

NUTRITION

Good source of

VC

Creamy hummus

The addition of yogurt makes this hummus deliciously creamy, and keeps the oil content lower than if made conventionally. Tahini is a thick, creamy paste made from ground sesame seeds. Light and dark varieties are available; the dark version is made from unhusked sesame seeds and has a much stronger, bitter flavour. For this recipe, it is preferable to use one of the lighter blends, but if you already have a jar of dark tahini in your cupboard, reduce the quantity to about 30ml (2 tbsp). Serve the hummus with toasted pitta breads, cucumber chunks and baby cherry tomatoes.

Serves 6

400g (14oz) can of chick peas, drained and rinsed	45ml (3 tbsp) lemon juice
1 garlic clove, skinned and crushed	45–60ml (3–4 level tbsp) Greek-style yogurt
75ml (3 fl oz) light tahini	salt and pepper
15ml (1 tbsp) olive oil	

Put the chick peas in a food processor or blender with the remaining ingredients and 25ml (1 fl oz) water. Blend until smooth, then taste and adjust the seasoning if necessary. Spoon the hummus into a dish, cover and chill for at least 20 minutes.

Tzatziki

Serve this as a dip with carrot sticks, corn chips or crisps and chunks of bread. It's also good on top of baked potatoes. Bio yogurt has a very mild flavour so it's my first choice for this recipe; if unavailable, use natural or Greek-style yogurt instead.

Makes about 300ml (½ pint)

¼ cucumber, finely chopped	1 garlic clove, skinned and crushed (optional)
about 300ml (½ pint) natural bio yogurt	1 spring onion, trimmed and finely chopped (optional)
30ml (2 level tbsp) chopped fresh mint or 2.5ml (½ tsp) concentrated mint sauce	salt and pepper

1 Mix the cucumber with the yogurt and fresh mint or mint sauce.

2 Stir in the garlic and spring onion, if using, and season with salt and pepper.

Red bean and cheese spread

Serve this speedily made spread with Oat crackers (see below) or wholemeal toast, or thin with a little fromage frais and serve as a dip with crudités.

Serves 6–8

1 small onion (preferably red), skinned and halved	125g (4oz) low-fat soft cheese
425g (15oz) can of red kidney beans, drained and rinsed	50g (2oz) vegetarian Cheddar cheese, coarsely grated
a squeeze of lemon juice	salt and pepper

1 Put the onion, beans and lemon juice in a blender or food processor and process until finely chopped. Add the cream cheese and process again until well mixed.

2 Turn the mixture into a bowl and fold in the Cheddar cheese. Season with salt and pepper, cover and leave to stand for at least 30 minutes to let the flavours develop.

Oat crackers

Crisp, savoury biscuits are surprisingly easy to make at home. If you have shaped cutters, use them to make the crackers more fun.

Makes about 30 small crackers

25g (1oz) plain white flour	125g (4oz) vegetable margarine or butter
125g (4oz) self-raising wholemeal flour	about 30–45ml (2–3 tbsp) milk
75g (3oz) porridge oats	
5ml (1 level tsp) salt	sesame seeds (optional)

1 Put the flours, oats and salt in a bowl and mix together. Rub in the margarine or butter, then gradually add enough milk to make a firm dough. Knead the mixture together lightly with your fingertips.

2 Roll out the dough on a lightly floured surface to 0.5cm (¼ inch) thick and cut out rounds with a 5.5cm (2¼ inch) biscuit cutter. Put the crackers on lightly greased baking sheets and sprinkle with sesame seeds, if using. Bake in the oven at 200°C (400°F) mark 6 for 10–15 minutes or until pale brown. Transfer to a wire rack and leave to cool.

Left to right: Red bean and cheese spread (above), Oat crackers (above), Guacamole (page 36)

Guacamole

Ripe avocados are essential to guacamole; a ripe avocado always 'gives' slightly when pressed at the pointed end. A hard, under-ripe fruit will ripen in 1–2 days at room temperature if stored in a fruit bowl with ripe fruit, or in about a week in the refrigerator. Serve guacamole with crudités and lower-salt crisps or corn chips.

Serves 8

1 small onion, skinned and quartered	10ml (2 level tsp) ground cumin
2–3 garlic cloves, skinned	5ml (1 level tsp) chilli powder or to taste
4 large ripe avocados	2 ripe tomatoes, seeded and roughly chopped
finely grated rind and juice of 2 small limes	salt and pepper
60ml (4 level tbsp) chopped fresh coriander	
10ml (2 level tsp) ground coriander	

1 Put the onion and garlic in a blender or food processor and process until finely chopped.

2 Halve, stone and peel the avocados, then chop roughly and add to the mixture with all the remaining ingredients, except the tomatoes and seasoning. Process until almost smooth.

3 Transfer the guacamole to a bowl and stir in the tomatoes. Season with salt and pepper. Cover and chill in the refrigerator for 30 minutes to let the flavours develop.

Mushroom pâté

Mushrooms are a great source of vegetable protein, but some children dislike their texture. A smooth pâté like this is therefore a good way to get them to eat mushrooms, but if they have disliked mushrooms in the past, it might be worth calling it 'vegetable' pâté! And then there's the problem of the 'green bits'. The chopped herbs in this recipe provide colour contrast, and of course they add flavour, but if you have someone in your family with an aversion to 'green bits', the herbs can be omitted.

Serves 6

25g (1oz) vegetable margarine or butter	a squeeze of lemon juice
450g (1lb) open-cup or field mushrooms, wiped and chopped	25g (1oz) ground hazelnuts or almonds
225g (8oz) button mushrooms, wiped and chopped	75g (3oz) vegetarian soft cheese with garlic and herbs, or plain soft cheese
1 garlic clove, skinned and crushed	30ml (2 level tbsp) chopped fresh chives
	salt and pepper

1 Heat the margarine or butter in a non-stick frying pan and sauté the mushrooms and garlic for 2–3 minutes or until beginning to soften. Add the lemon juice, then lower the heat and cook for about 10 minutes or until the mushrooms are tender. Sprinkle with the ground nuts and cook over a high heat for a further 2 minutes, stirring. Leave to cool slightly.

2 Purée the mixture in a blender or food processor with the soft cheese. Add the chives and season with salt and pepper. Leave to cool completely before serving.

NUTRITION

Good source of

VB$_2$

Tacos

Crispy corn taco shells are available in packets from large supermarkets. They make a change from bread and rolls and can be used in much the same way –
although the filling can be piled much higher. Apart from the filling suggested here, try Guacamole (see page 36), Creamy hummus (see page 33), egg mayonnaise, or any salad ingredients.

Serves 6

6 tacos or 6 small pitta breads	2 tomatoes, chopped
15ml (1 tbsp) vegetable oil	chopped fresh coriander (optional)
1 red pepper, seeded and finely chopped	salt and pepper
1 onion, skinned and finely chopped	shredded lettuce and soured cream or Greek-style yogurt, to serve
1 garlic clove, skinned and crushed	
425g (15oz) can of red kidney, black-eyed or other beans, drained and rinsed	

1 Warm the tacos in the oven according to the packet instructions. If using pitta breads, arrange them in a single layer on a baking sheet and heat in the oven at 200°C (400°F) mark 6 for 5–10 minutes or until puffed up. Cut in half widthways.

2 Meanwhile, heat the oil in a non-stick frying pan and cook the pepper, onion and garlic for 5–10 minutes or until softened. Tip the beans into a bowl and mash with a potato masher until broken up and slightly mashed.

3 Add the beans and tomatoes to the softened vegetables, and cook over a high heat for a few minutes. Add the coriander and season with salt and pepper. Pile into the tacos or pitta breads and top with shredded lettuce and a spoonful of soured cream or Greek-style yogurt.

NUTRITION

Good source of

F **I** **VC**

Cheese scones

Scones are quick to throw together at a moment's notice. Serve them as an accompaniment to salads and soups, or split and filled with salad, yeast extract, cheese or hummus. They really are best served fresh and warm from the oven but any leftover scones could be filled and included in a lunchbox the following day.

Makes about 12

225g (8oz) self-raising white flour, or a mixture of half white and half wholemeal flour	5ml (1 level tsp) baking powder
a pinch of salt	40g (1½oz) vegetable margarine or butter
5ml (1 level tsp) mustard powder	125g (4oz) vegetarian Cheddar cheese, grated
	about 150ml (¼ pint) milk

1 Grease a baking sheet. Sift the flour, salt, mustard powder and baking powder together into a bowl. Rub in the margarine or butter until the mixture resembles breadcrumbs. Stir in three quarters of the cheese and enough milk to give a fairly soft, light dough.

2 On a lightly floured surface, roll out the dough to about 2cm (¾ inch) thick and cut into rounds with a 5cm (2 inch) plain cutter. Put on the baking sheet, brush the tops with milk and sprinkle with the remaining cheese.

3 Bake in the oven at 220°C (425°F) mark 7 for about 10 minutes or until risen and golden. Serve warm.

VARIATIONS

Nut Scones Omit the mustard. The cheese may be omitted or left in, as preferred. Add 50g (2oz) finely chopped mixed nuts to the rubbed-in ingredients. Sprinkle the scones with sesame or poppy seeds before baking.

Plain Scones To make plain scones, for serving with jam and cream, follow the basic recipe but omit the herbs, cheese and mustard (but you still add salt, even to sweet scones).

Sweet Fruit Scones Add 50g (2oz) dried mixed fruit to a Plain Scone mixture before adding the milk.

Welsh rarebit

There's nothing wrong with old-fashioned favourites like this! Use a heavy-based, non-stick pan to prevent the mixture sticking.

Serves 2

125g (4oz) vegetarian Cheddar cheese, grated	30ml (2 tbsp) brown ale or milk
a pinch of mustard powder	1 tomato
salt and pepper	2 thick slices of bread

1 Put all the ingredients, except the tomato and bread, in a small heavy-based, non-stick saucepan and heat very gently until the cheese has melted.

2 Meanwhile, thickly slice the tomato and toast the bread on one side. Place the bread, untoasted side up, on two heatproof serving plates.

3 Arrange the tomato slices on the bread and pour the cheese mixture over the top. Cook under a hot grill until golden and bubbling. Serve at once.

NUTRITION

Good source of

C P VA

Cheese puffs

These delectable puffs are meant to be served cold filled with egg mayonnaise, hummus, cream cheese and celery or guacamole, but they are so moreish that it's hard to resist eating them warm straight from the oven just as they are.

Makes about 16

65g (2½oz) plain white flour	2 free-range eggs, beaten
a pinch of salt	125g (4oz) Gruyère cheese, cut into small cubes
50g (2oz) vegetable margarine or butter	grated Parmesan cheese (optional)
150ml (¼ pint) water	

1 Sift the flour and salt on to a plate. Put the margarine or butter and water into a saucepan and heat gently until the fat has melted. Once it has melted, bring the mixture quickly to the boil, then remove from the heat and tip in the flour. Beat thoroughly

with a wooden spoon until the mixture forms a ball in the centre of the pan. Leave to cool for 1–2 minutes.

2 Beat in the eggs, a little at a time, until the mixture is smooth and fairly soft but still holds its shape. Fold in the Gruyère cheese.

3 Put heaped spoonfuls of the mixture on to a wetted baking sheet, sprinkle with a little Parmesan, if using, and bake in the oven at 200°C (400°F) mark 6 for about 20 minutes or until well risen and golden brown. Remove from the oven, slit each puff with a sharp knife to let the steam escape, then return to the oven for a further 5 minutes to dry out. Cool on a wire rack. When cold, fill with your chosen filling and serve at once.

Spinach and cheese blinis

Serve these savoury breakfast pancakes with wedges of tomato sprinkled with a little vegetarian feta cheese, or with a spoonful of Creamy hummus (see page 33).

Serves 4–6

450g (1lb) spinach, trimmed	50g (2oz) vegetarian Cheddar cheese, grated
75g (3oz) plain white flour	salt and pepper
5ml (1 level tsp) baking powder	olive or vegetable oil for frying
2 free-range eggs	
1 garlic clove, skinned and crushed	

1 Wash the spinach in plenty of cold running water, then put it in a heavy-based saucepan with just the water clinging to the leaves. Cover tightly and cook for 2–3 minutes or until just wilted. Drain and squeeze dry, then chop roughly and tip into a mixing bowl.

2 Add the remaining ingredients, except the olive or vegetable oil, to the chopped spinach and mix well to make a smooth, fairly stiff batter.

3 To fry the blinis, heat a little oil in a large heavy-based frying pan. Drop large tablespoonfuls of the batter into the oil and fry for 2–3 minutes on each side or until golden brown. As the blinis cook, remove them from the pan and keep them warm while frying the remainder. Serve warm.

NUTRITION

Good source of

VA   VC

Cowboy beans

This makes a change from beans on toast, and it doesn't take much effort once you've assembled the ingredients. To make a more elaborate dish, you could mix a few sautéed vegetables, such as peppers, mushrooms, courgettes and sweetcorn, with the beans.

Serves 4

425g (15oz) can of red kidney beans, drained and rinsed	2.5ml (½ level tsp) baking powder
425g (15oz) can of baked beans	15ml (1 tbsp) vegetable oil
50g (2oz) self-raising white flour	75g (3oz) vegetarian Cheddar cheese, grated
50g (2oz) cornmeal	75ml (3 fl oz) milk
1.25ml (¼ level tsp) salt	2 free-range eggs, separated

1 Tip the two cans of beans into a gratin or baking dish and mix together.
2 Put all the other ingredients, except the egg whites, in a bowl and beat together to make a fairly stiff batter. Add a little extra milk if necessary. Whisk the egg whites until stiff and fold into the batter.

3 Spoon the mixture on top of the beans (it should almost cover them, but don't worry if a few are still visible) and bake in the oven at 200°C (400°F) mark 6 for about 20 minutes or until the topping is golden brown and well risen.

NUTRITION

Good source of

F   P   C

PACKED LUNCH IDEAS

Chick pea bites

A simplified version of *felafel* (Middle Eastern patties made from chick peas or beans), these are good served in pitta bread with *tabbouleh* (bulgar wheat salad). They can also be eaten warm, topped with a spoonful of natural yogurt.

Makes about 16

125g (4oz) chick peas, soaked overnight in cold water, or one 425g (15oz) can of chick peas, drained and rinsed	15ml (1 tbsp) mild curry paste
	30ml (2 tbsp) peanut butter
1 onion, skinned and roughly chopped	125g (4oz) wholemeal breadcrumbs
1 garlic clove, skinned	1 egg
	salt and pepper
45ml (3 tbsp) tahini (see page 33)	oil for frying or baking

1 If using dried chick peas, drain them, put them in a saucepan and cover with fresh water. Bring to the boil, then reduce the heat and simmer for 1½–2 hours or until tender. Drain well.

2 Put the cooked or canned chick peas in a food processor with all the remaining ingredients, except the seasoning and oil, and process until well mixed and almost smooth. Season with salt and pepper.

3 Shape the mixture into about 16 small balls with your hands. Fry in hot oil, turning frequently, for 3–4 minutes or until golden brown, then drain on absorbent kitchen paper. Alternatively, arrange on a greased baking sheet, brush lightly with oil and cook in the oven at 180°C (350°F) mark 4 for about 30 minutes or until golden brown. Leave to cool completely before using to fill pitta breads and packing in a lunchbox.

NUTRITION

Good source of

P

44

Mushroom pies

Yogurt pastry is quick to make and easy to handle; this is a good recipe to get the children to help with.

Makes about 8

15ml (1 tbsp) vegetable oil	125g (4oz) vegetable margarine or butter
225g (8oz) button mushrooms, wiped and fairly finely chopped	1 free-range egg
1 garlic clove, skinned and crushed (optional)	150ml (5 fl oz) Greek-style yogurt
50g (2oz) frozen petits pois	300g (11oz) self-raising white flour
2 spring onions, trimmed and chopped	milk for brushing
45ml (3 tbsp) mayonnaise	ground hazelnuts or almonds (optional)
salt and pepper	

1 Heat the oil in a frying pan and sauté the mushrooms and garlic, if using, for about 5 minutes or until soft. Add the petits pois and cook for a few minutes more. Add the spring onions, mayonnaise and seasoning, and mix well. Remove from the heat and leave to cool.

2 To make the pastry, melt the margarine or butter and leave to cool. Whisk the egg into the yogurt until thoroughly mixed, then gradually pour in the melted margarine or butter. Put the flour and 5ml (1 level tsp) salt in a bowl, make a well in the centre and gradually add the yogurt mixture. Beat together to make a soft dough.

3 Turn the dough on to a lightly floured surface and knead for a few minutes until smooth. Roll out very thinly and cut out about eight 10cm (4 inch) rounds using a small plate or bowl as a guide. Reroll the trimmings and cut out more rounds, as necessary.

4 Divide the mushroom filling between half of the pastry rounds. Brush the edges with a little milk, then place a second pastry circle on top of each. Press together to seal in the filling. Crimp the edges, brush with a little more milk and sprinkle with ground nuts, if using.

5 Transfer the pies to a baking sheet and cook in the oven at 200°C (400°F) mark 6 for about 15 minutes or until golden brown. Leave to cool completely before wrapping and packing in a lunchbox.

Vegetable empanadillas

Based on a Spanish recipe, these tasty little pies are deep-fried. This produces deliciously crisp pastries which are well worth the effort of making them.

Makes about 16

25g (1oz) vegetable margarine or butter	1 tomato, finely chopped
15ml (1 tbsp) olive oil	2 spring onions, trimmed and finely chopped
165g (5½oz) plain white flour	25g (1oz) sultanas
salt and pepper	30ml (2 tbsp) red pesto (optional)
1 free-range egg yolk	milk for brushing
1 hard-boiled free-range egg, finely chopped	vegetable oil for deep-frying

1 Put the margarine or butter, olive oil and 75ml (3 fl oz) water in a small saucepan. Heat until the fat has melted and the water is just boiling. Remove from the heat, then quickly add the flour and 2.5ml (½ level tsp) salt all at once. Beat vigorously with a wooden spoon, then beat in the egg yolk.

2 Turn the dough on to a floured surface and knead briefly until smooth and elastic. Cover with a clean, damp tea-towel and leave to rest at room temperature for 30 minutes.

3 To make the filling, mix together the remaining ingredients, except the milk and oil, and season with salt and pepper.

4 Roll out the pastry on a lightly floured surface and cut out 7.5cm (3 inch) rounds using a pastry cutter. Reroll the pastry trimmings as necessary until you have cut out about 16 rounds. Divide the filling between the pastry rounds, placing it on one half of each round. Brush the edges of the pastry with milk, then fold the other half of each pastry round over the filling and press the edges together to seal.

5 Heat the oil in a deep-fat fryer to 190°C (375°F) or until a cube of bread dropped into the oil turns brown in 30 seconds. Fry the empanadillas in batches for 2–3 minutes or until golden brown. Drain on crumpled absorbent kitchen paper and leave to cool.

Ratatouille parcels

These are quick and easy to make with ready-made pastry. However, if you prefer to make your own pastry, you will need about 350g (12oz) shortcrust – wholemeal is particularly good with this filling (see page 120).

Makes 4

1 small red pepper, seeded and chopped	**225g (8oz) tomatoes, chopped**
1 onion, skinned and roughly chopped	**salt and pepper**
1 large courgette, trimmed and roughly chopped	**370g (13oz) packet of puff or flaky pastry, thawed if frozen**
1 very small aubergine, trimmed and roughly chopped	**milk or beaten free-range egg for brushing**
1 garlic clove, skinned and crushed	**sesame and poppy seeds for sprinkling (optional)**

1 To make the ratatouille, put the chopped vegetables, garlic and tomatoes in a saucepan. Season and cook over a gentle heat for about 25 minutes or until the vegetables are softened and most of the liquid has evaporated. If the mixture looks very wet, boil it rapidly until reduced. Remove from the heat and leave to cool.

2 Roll out the pastry on a lightly floured surface into a 40.5cm (16 inch) square. Using a sharp knife, cut into four smaller squares. Trim the edges and reserve the trimmings for decoration.

3 Put the pastry squares on two baking sheets. Spoon a quarter of the ratatouille in the centre of each pastry square. Brush the pastry edges with milk or beaten egg, then bring the four points of each square together over the filling. Pinch and seal the edges together to make four envelope-shaped parcels.

4 If you have time, decorate the parcels with the pastry trimmings. Make a small hole in the centre of each parcel to let steam escape. Brush with milk or beaten egg to glaze, then sprinkle with a mixture of sesame and poppy seeds, if liked. Bake in the oven at 220°C (425°F) mark 7 for 15–20 minutes or until golden brown and well risen. Leave to cool completely before wrapping and packing in a lunchbox.

NUTRITION

Good source of

VC

Potato salad

Encourage your children to eat new potatoes with the skins on. Spoon the potato salad into a small rigid container or cleaned yogurt pot for including in a packed lunch.

Serves 6

700g (1½lb) small new potatoes, washed	75ml (5 tbsp) mayonnaise
salt and pepper	3 spring onions, trimmed and chopped
225ml (8 fl oz) fromage frais or natural yogurt	

1 Cook the potatoes in boiling salted water for 10–15 minutes or until tender. Drain thoroughly and leave to cool. Cut each potato in half or, for younger children or if the potatoes aren't really small, cut them into quarters. Put the potatoes in a large mixing bowl.

2 Beat together the remaining ingredients. Pour over the potatoes and toss together to coat thoroughly.

VARIATIONS

Curried Potato Salad Omit the spring onion. Add 10ml (2 level tsp) mild curry paste, 1 small crushed garlic clove, and a handful of sultanas to the mayonnaise mixture.

Green Bean and Potato Salad Add a handful of lightly cooked green beans to the salad. Flavour the mayonnaise mixture with 15ml (1 tbsp) tahini (see page 33). Sprinkle with a few toasted sesame seeds.

Waldorf salad

Choose a crisp lettuce, such as cos, for this classic salad, and scatter it on top of the other ingredients once they're packed ready for transporting; if you mix everything together, the lettuce will be soggy by lunchtime.

Serves 4–6

2 eating apples	150ml (¼ pint) mayonnaise
juice of ½ lemon	salt and pepper
3 celery sticks, trimmed	a few cos lettuce leaves
50g (2oz) walnut pieces, chopped	

1 Core and roughly chop the apples. Toss in the lemon juice. Cut the celery into chunks and mix with the apple and walnuts.

2 Add the mayonnaise to the apple mixture and toss together. Season lightly.

3 Transfer the salad to a rigid container. Tear the lettuce into rough pieces and scatter on top. Cover and store in the refrigerator until ready to transport.

Pasta salad

Another salad that travels well in a lunchbox. Choose medium-sized pasta shapes to give the salad some 'bite'.

Serves 6

175g (6oz) pasta shapes	1 hard-boiled egg, chopped
salt and pepper	150ml (5 fl oz) fromage frais
15ml (1 tbsp) vegetable oil	10ml (2 level tsp) mild curry paste
1 ripe mango	10ml (2 tsp) runny honey
a handful of fresh spinach, trimmed and thoroughly washed	
125g (4oz) soaked and cooked dried borlotti beans (see page 12) or half a 425g (15oz) can of borlotti beans, drained and rinsed	

1 Cook the pasta in boiling salted water until just tender. Drain and rinse with boiling water. Drain again, then tip into a mixing bowl and toss with the vegetable oil.

2 To prepare the mango, cut the fruit away from either side of the central stone in two large slices. Make a series of lengthways, then crossways cuts in the flesh of each piece without cutting through the skin. Push the skin inside out to expose the cubes of flesh, then cut them off. Peel the remaining central section of fruit surrounding the stone and cut away from the stone in cubes.

3 Mix the mango with the pasta. Finely shred the spinach and add to the pasta with the beans and egg. Mix together the fromage frais, curry paste and honey, season with salt and pepper, and pour over the salad. Toss everything together well.

NUTRITION

Good source of

VC

Picnic eggs

These are a vegetarian alternative to scotch eggs – and much tastier too! Don't forget that egg consumption should be restricted to about three per week and that the eggs should be free-range.

Makes 4

5 free-range eggs	175g (6oz) fresh wholemeal breadcrumbs
15ml (1 tbsp) vegetable oil	salt and pepper
1 parsnip, peeled and grated	seasoned flour
1 large carrot, peeled and grated	sesame seeds (optional)
2 spring onions, trimmed and finely chopped	vegetable oil for brushing

1 Put four of the eggs in a saucepan, cover with cold water and bring to the boil, then reduce the heat and simmer for 5 minutes. Drain and rinse with plenty of cold running water until cool enough to handle, then carefully peel off the shells.

2 To make the coating, heat the oil in a saucepan, add the parsnip and carrot, and fry until soft. Add the spring onions, breadcrumbs and salt and pepper to taste, and remove from the heat. Beat the remaining egg and add enough of it to the breadcrumb mixture to make a soft, dough-like mixture.

3 Divide the mixture into four. Take one portion and knead it with wetted hands, then flatten it into a thick pancake. Coat one of the hard-boiled eggs in a little seasoned flour, then place it on top of the coating 'pancake'. Mould the coating around the egg to enclose it completely. Repeat with the remaining coating mixture and eggs. Coat the eggs in a few sesame seeds, if liked, pressing them on with your fingertips.

4 Put the eggs on a greased baking sheet. Lightly brush with oil and bake in the oven at 190°C (375°F) mark 5 for about 20 minutes or until golden brown and firm to the touch. Serve cold.

NUTRITION

Good source of

P   VB₁₂

Clockwise from top: Rice salad (page 52), Malted sultana loaf (page 116), Picnic eggs (above)

Rice salad

This is one of those salads with endless possible permutations. You could add a few cooked red kidney beans, chopped nuts, sunflower or sesame seeds, chopped dried fruit, orange segments, chopped fresh pineapple, or virtually any salad ingredient that you have to hand, avoiding tomatoes because they tend to make the salad too soggy. As for the dressing, the pesto is optional, but my family likes it – you could add a crushed garlic clove instead. Store the salad in cleaned yogurt pots, or cottage cheese or margarine cartons in the refrigerator, ready to be added to a lunchbox. Don't forget to put in a fork or spoon, too.

Serves 6

175g (6oz) long-grain white or brown rice	60ml (4 tbsp) sweetcorn kernels (fresh, frozen or canned)
salt and pepper	75ml (5 tbsp) olive oil
½ small red pepper, seeded and chopped	30ml (2 tbsp) lemon juice
50g (2oz) fine green beans, trimmed and roughly chopped	30ml (2 tbsp) pesto (optional)

1 Cook the rice in boiling salted water for about 10 minutes if cooking white rice, or about 25 minutes for brown rice, or until it is tender. Drain thoroughly and rinse with boiling water. Tip into a bowl, fluff up the grains with a fork and leave to cool.

2 Cook the red pepper, green beans and fresh or frozen sweetcorn, if using, in boiling salted water until just tender. Drain and rinse with cold water. Drain well and mix with the rice. If using canned sweetcorn, it can be drained and added straight to the rice.

3 Whisk together the oil, lemon juice and pesto. Season with a little salt and pepper, and pour over the rice mixture. Toss everything together to coat with the dressing.

NUTRITION

Good source of

VC

Coleslaw

As a result of recent salmonella scares, homemade mayonnaise made with raw eggs is not recommended for young children. However, commercially prepared mayonnaise is safe, because although it still contains raw eggs, they have been pasteurised. Look out for brands made with free-range eggs in health food shops. For packed lunches, this coleslaw can be used as a sandwich or pitta bread filling, or spooned into rigid containers to be eaten with a fork.

Serves 6

225g (8oz) white cabbage, trimmed and finely shredded	a handful of fresh parsley, chopped (optional)
1 small carrot, peeled and coarsely grated	about 150ml (5 fl oz) mayonnaise or a mixture of natural yogurt and mayonnaise
1 small onion, skinned and very thinly sliced	
	salt and pepper

1 Mix together all the vegetables and the parsley, if using, then add enough mayonnaise to moisten the mixture.

2 Season the coleslaw with salt and pepper, cover and chill in the refrigerator for a few hours before using.

NUTRITION

Good source of

VC

VARIATIONS

Cheese Coleslaw Add 3 chopped spring onions to the vegetable mixture. Coarsely grate 75g (3oz) strongly flavoured vegetarian Cheddar cheese and fold in after adding the mayonnaise.

Fruit and Nut Coleslaw Add 75g (3oz) mixed unsalted peanuts and raisins with a few chopped no-need-to-soak dried apricots. Flavour the mayonnaise with 5–10ml (1–2 tsp) mild curry paste.

Apple Coleslaw Core and chop or coarsely grate 1 red apple (with the skin on if your children like it) and toss in a little lemon juice. Drain thoroughly, then blend with the remaining ingredients. Sprinkle with a few toasted sesame seeds.

Sandwich or roll fillings

Any of the wide range of hard and soft vegetarian cheeses now available make good
nutritious sandwich fillings, especially if combined with salad ingredients.
Others include egg mayonnaise, peanut butter, yeast extract, hummus, and any of the
spreads or pâtés on pages 33–7. Don't forget that you can ring the changes
with the breads as well as the fillings. Try seed and multigrain breads and rolls as well as
pitta breads, bagels, French bread, croissants, rye bread or oatmeal bread.
It doesn't always have to be wholemeal either; in fact very young children will find
dense wholemeal bread too filling.
Apart from the usual combinations, try these suggestions:

Banana and Date Mash a ripe banana
with a squeeze of lemon juice and mix
with a few finely chopped stoned dates.

Chocolate and Nut Spread Spread
straight from the jar! Hazelnuts are high in
protein so this spread makes a nutritious
occasional treat.

Avocado Mash a ripe avocado with a
squeeze of lemon juice, a chopped spring
onion, a spoonful of mayonnaise and seasoning. Arrange iceberg lettuce on the
bread and top with the avocado mixture.

Tahini and Cream Cheese Blend a little
tahini (see page 33) with some cream
cheese. Spread thickly on to bread and top

with slices of cucumber and a few seedless
grape halves. Season with lots of black
pepper.

Yeast Extract and Cottage Cheese
Thinly spread buttered bread with yeast
extract. Cover with cottage cheese and
with watercress, if liked.

Greek Salad Mix chopped tomato,
crumbled feta cheese, a little chopped
onion and a few chopped stoned olives.

Tomato and Mozzarella Cover the
bread with thinly sliced tomato, sliced
mozzarella and a few fresh basil leaves, if
available. Season with salt and plenty of
black pepper.

MAIN COURSE DISHES

Veggie bangers

Instead of tomato sauce, serve these sausages with a salsa made from finely chopped tomatoes, spring onions, cucumber and herbs, moistened with a few drops of vinegar and a splash of olive oil. Season with a sprinkling of sugar and salt and pepper.

Makes 6

50g (2oz) vegetable margarine or butter	125g (4oz) medium oatmeal
225g (8oz) onions, skinned and finely chopped	125g (4oz) ground mixed nuts
225g (8oz) leeks, trimmed, washed and finely sliced	1 free-range egg, beaten
5ml (1 level tsp) dried sage	salt and pepper
125g (4oz) fresh breadcrumbs	vegetable oil for cooking

1 Heat the margarine or butter in a frying pan, add the onions and leeks, and cook over a low heat until softened. Add all the remaining ingredients, except the oil, and mix thoroughly together. Leave until completely cool.

2 Shape the mixture into 6 large fat sausages.

3 Heat a little oil in a frying pan, add the sausages and cook until browned on all sides. Alternatively, place the sausages on a baking sheet and brush lightly with oil. Cook in the oven at 200°C (400°F) mark 6 for about 25 minutes or until brown. Serve hot.

NUTRITION

Good source of

F   VC

Curried eggs

The eggs and the sauce can be prepared in advance. Simply reheat the sauce just before serving and pour over the eggs. You could also add a few slices of banana to the sauce. Serve with chunks of cucumber and plenty of pitta or nan bread to mop up the sauce.

Serves 4

15ml (1 tbsp) vegetable oil	15ml (1 tbsp) mango chutney
1 garlic clove, skinned and crushed	25g (1oz) creamed coconut, chopped
1 onion, skinned and chopped	15ml (1 tbsp) tomato purée
10ml (2 level tsp) mild curry paste	salt and pepper
50g (2oz) split red lentils	4 hard-boiled free-range eggs
1 eating apple, peeled, cored and grated	

1 Heat the oil in a saucepan and sauté the garlic and onion for about 5 minutes or until softened. Add the curry paste and lentils, and cook for 2 minutes. Add all the remaining ingredients, except the eggs, and 300ml (½ pint) water. Bring to the boil, then lower the heat, cover and simmer for about 20 minutes or until the lentils are very soft and mushy. Beat thoroughly.

2 Shell the eggs and cut in half (or chop roughly for smaller children). Pour the sauce over the eggs and serve.

NUTRITION

Good source of

VA   VC

Mild vegetable curry with banana raita

I find that this mild, creamy curry is acceptable to most children. However, if your children are real curry lovers, they may prefer a more authentic, fiery sauce. Simply omit the curry paste and use 5ml (1 level tsp) each of ground cumin, coriander and chilli powder (or fresh chilli to taste) and 2.5ml (½ tsp) ground fenugreek. Fry the spices with the garlic. Serve the curry with boiled rice and cooling banana raita.

Serves 6

15ml (1 tbsp) vegetable oil	225g (8oz) soaked and cooked dried black-eyed beans (see page 12) or one 425g (15oz) can of black-eyed beans, drained and rinsed (optional)
2 garlic cloves, skinned and crushed	
50g (2oz) split red lentils	
45ml (3 tbsp) instant coconut milk powder	125g (4oz) shelled fresh or frozen peas
15ml (1 level tbsp) mild curry paste	150ml (5 fl oz) natural bio yogurt
salt and pepper	FOR THE BANANA RAITA
225g (8oz) potato, peeled and roughly chopped	300ml (½ pint) natural bio yogurt
225g (8oz) carrot, peeled and thickly sliced	1 banana
1 small cauliflower, broken into florets	15ml (1 tbsp) lime juice
	30ml (2 level tbsp) chopped fresh coriander
175g (6oz) green beans, trimmed and cut in half	salt and pepper

1 Heat the oil in a large saucepan, add the garlic and lentils, and cook for 2 minutes, stirring all the time. Add the coconut milk powder, the curry paste, salt and pepper and 300ml (½ pint) water. Bring to the boil, then lower the heat, cover the pan and simmer gently for about 15 minutes or until the lentils are very soft. Beat vigorously to make a fairly smooth sauce.

2 Add all the vegetables, except frozen peas (if using), cover the pan and simmer for a further 20 minutes or until the vegetables are tender. Add frozen peas (if using) and cook for a few minutes more until tender. Stir in the yogurt, and season.

3 Make the raita just before serving. Put the yogurt in a bowl. Peel the banana, slice fairly thinly and toss in the lime juice. Carefully fold into the yogurt with the coriander. Season with salt and pepper.

NUTRITION

Good source of

F   VA   VC

Rice and peas with plantain chips

Top this effortlessly simple dish with natural yogurt and a spoonful of grated cheese
before sprinkling with the plantain chips – these aren't essential but they
are delicious. If you can't find plantains (look out for them in large supermarkets or
Afro-Caribbean stores), you could use green bananas.

Serves 4

175g (6oz) long-grain or basmati rice	3 ripe, juicy tomatoes, roughly chopped
salt and pepper	a large knob of vegetable margarine or butter
125g (4oz) shelled fresh or frozen peas	FOR THE PLANTAIN CHIPS
175g (6oz) soaked and cooked dried aduki beans (see page 12) or one 425g (15oz) can of beans of your choice, drained and rinsed	1 plantain
	vegetable oil for deep-frying

1 Cook the rice in a large saucepan of boiling salted water until almost tender.

2 Meanwhile, make the plantain chips. Peel the plantain and cut into fairly thin slices. Deep-fry in hot oil in small batches for 4–5 minutes or until tender and pale golden brown. Drain on absorbent kitchen paper.

3 When the rice is almost cooked, add the peas and continue cooking until the peas and rice are tender. Drain and return to the pan with the beans and tomatoes.

4 Add the margarine or butter, cover the pan with a tightly fitting lid and cook for a few minutes to heat through. Season with pepper and a little extra salt, if necessary, then serve as suggested above with the warm plantain chips.

Vegetable lasagne

If using precooked dried lasagne sheets, add a little extra liquid (stock or water) to the vegetable mixture and omit step 2 of the method. Lasagne is traditionally layered with béchamel sauce, but I like to use mascarpone cheese to save time and effort. If you prefer to make it the traditional way, see the variation given opposite.

Serves 8

30ml (2 tbsp) olive oil	two 400g (14oz) cans of chopped tomatoes
1 garlic clove, skinned and crushed	30ml (2 tbsp) tomato purée
1 large onion, skinned and chopped	salt and pepper
225g (8oz) mushrooms, wiped and sliced	about 350g (12oz) fresh or 225g (8oz) dried lasagne
1 large red pepper, seeded and chopped	about 30ml (2 tbsp) milk
4 courgettes, chopped	350g (12oz) mascarpone
5ml (1 level tsp) dried marjoram	grated Parmesan or vegetarian Cheddar cheese (optional)

1 Heat the oil in a large saucepan, add the vegetables and cook over a high heat for a few minutes, stirring all the time. Add the marjoram, canned tomatoes, tomato purée and plenty of salt and pepper. Bring to the boil, then lower the heat, cover and simmer for 20 minutes.

2 Meanwhile, if using dried lasagne, cook it in boiling water according to the packet instructions. Drain and leave to dry on a clean tea-towel.

3 Spoon about half of the vegetable mixture in the base of a 2.8 litre (5 pint) ovenproof dish. Cover with a layer of lasagne. Repeat the layers, ending with a layer of lasagne that covers the vegetables completely.

4 Beat the milk into the mascarpone to make it spreadable, adding a little extra if necessary. Spoon on top of the lasagne, season with salt and pepper and sprinkle with the cheese, if using. Bake in the oven at 200°C (400°F) mark 6 for 40–45 minutes or until golden brown. Leave to cool and settle for about 15 minutes before cutting.

NUTRITION

Good source of

VC

VARIATIONS

Spinach and Bean Lasagne Omit the courgettes and red pepper from the main-recipe. Add 450g (1lb) washed and trimmed fresh spinach and a 425g (15oz) can of black-eyed beans, drained and rinsed, to the vegetable mixture towards the end of the cooking time. Assemble and bake as opposite.

Leek and Gruyère Lasagne Omit the onion, red pepper and mushrooms from the main recipe. Add 700g (1½lb) washed, trimmed and thinly sliced leeks, 225g (8oz) grated Gruyère cheese and 150ml (¼ pint)

soured cream to the vegetable mixture. Sprinkle the top with a little extra Gruyère instead of Parmesan or Cheddar. Assemble and bake as opposite.

Béchamel Lasagne Make 900ml (1½ pints) béchamel sauce following the recipe on page 122. Spoon a little on top of the vegetable mixture, but save most for the top. Omit the mascarpone and instead pour the béchamel sauce over the last layer of pasta to cover it completely. Sprinkle with cheese, if using, and bake as opposite.

Nut burgers

I find that cashew nuts are the best choice for burgers for kids because they have a slightly softer texture and sweeter flavour than many of the other varieties.

Makes 8

50g (2oz) vegetable margarine or butter	30ml (2 level tbsp) chopped fresh parsley, coriander or chives (optional)
2 onions, skinned and chopped	175g (6oz) fresh breadcrumbs
1 garlic clove, skinned and crushed	15ml (1 tbsp) light soy sauce
125g (4oz) mushrooms, wiped and finely chopped	1 egg, beaten
1 carrot, peeled and grated	pepper
125g (4oz) cashew nuts, finely chopped	vegetable oil for cooking

1 Heat the margarine or butter in a frying pan, add the onion, garlic, mushrooms and carrot, and cook over a low heat until softened. Add the remaining ingredients, except the oil. Divide the mixture into 8 and shape each portion into a burger.

2 Heat a little oil in a frying pan and cook the burgers for 3–4 minutes on each side or until golden brown. Alternatively, brush the burgers with a little oil and cook under a hot grill.

Quick pasta gratin

This is another dish that came about by accident when faced with hungry children, a few leftover vegetables and not much else in the cupboard. Use whatever vegetables you have to hand – sweetcorn, peas and cherry tomatoes would all work well. If you don't have any flavoured cream cheese, use plain instead, or you could use mascarpone.

Serves 2–3

225g (8oz) pasta shapes	about 125g (4oz) cream cheese with garlic and herbs
salt and pepper	60ml (4 tbsp) milk
½ orange, green or red pepper, seeded and roughly chopped	30ml (2 tbsp) freshly grated Parmesan or vegetarian Cheddar cheese
a few green beans or mangetouts	30ml (2 tbsp) breadcrumbs
1–2 tomatoes, quartered	
a handful of fresh spinach leaves, trimmed and washed	

1 Cook the pasta in a large saucepan of boiling salted water, adding the chopped pepper and green beans or mangetouts for the last 5 minutes of cooking. Drain thoroughly and tip back into the saucepan.

2 Quickly add the tomatoes, spinach, cream cheese and milk, and toss everything together, stirring until the cheese melts and the spinach wilts. If the cheese refuses to melt, turn the heat on low for a minute or so. It should just coat the pasta and vegetables; add a little more if it seems too dry. Season with salt and pepper.

3 Turn the mixture into a shallow heatproof dish and sprinkle with the Parmesan or Cheddar cheese and the breadcrumbs. Cook under a hot grill until brown.

NUTRITION

Good source of

VA   **VC**

Mixed vegetable tart

For speed, I don't usually bother to bake the pastry case before adding the filling. If you prefer your pastry to be absolutely crisp, however, bake the empty pastry case blind in the oven at 200°C (400°F) mark 6 for about 10 minutes, then remove the paper and baking beans and cook for a further 5 minutes.

Serves 8

1 quantity Wholemeal pastry or one of the other variations given on pages 120–21	a handful of fresh herbs, finely chopped (optional)
	300ml (½ pint) milk
1 red or green pepper, seeded and roughly chopped	2 free-range eggs
175g (6oz) small broccoli florets	salt and pepper
2 small firm tomatoes, quartered	

1 On a lightly floured surface, roll out the pastry and use to line a shallow 23cm (9 inch) flan tin with a loose bottom. Stand the tin on a baking sheet.

2 Blanch the red or green pepper in boiling water for 1 minute. Drain thoroughly, then arrange in the pastry case with the remaining vegetables and the herbs. Beat together the milk and eggs, and season with salt and pepper. Pour over the vegetables to just below the top of the pastry case.

3 Bake the tart in the oven at 200°C (400°F) mark 6 for about 30 minutes or until just set. Serve warm or cold.

NUTRITION

Good source of

VA   VC

VARIATIONS

Bean and Vegetable Tart Sprinkle the vegetables with about 50g (2oz) cooked or canned beans, such as aduki beans, black-eyed beans or cannellini beans.

Baby Corn and Tomato Tart Omit the broccoli. Replace the tomatoes with a few firm cherry tomatoes. Blanch 125g (4oz) baby corn cobs with the pepper. Arrange the corn in the pastry case so that the ends stick up out of the custard.

Courgette and Pesto Tart Replace the broccoli with thickly sliced courgettes. Add 30ml (2 tbsp) pesto to the milk and egg mixture.

Mushroom Tart Replace all the vegetables with 350g (12oz) halved button mushrooms, sautéed until just tender in 30ml (2 tbsp) vegetable oil with 1 skinned and crushed garlic clove.

Cheese and Vegetable Tart Add 75g (3oz) grated vegetarian Cheddar cheese to the custard and sprinkle the tart generously with Cheddar or Parmesan cheese before baking.

Barbecue burgers

Look out for ready-to-eat vegetarian mince (Textured Vegetable Protein) in freezer cabinets in health food shops. It can be cooked from frozen and is surprisingly good. The only problem with making burgers with it is that it doesn't stick together like meat mince, so you will need to add an egg to bind it. Smoky Barbecue Sauce is available from larger supermarkets and delicatessens; you can use tomato ketchup as a substitute but the flavour won't be so good – to compensate, add a splash of vegetarian Worcester sauce, too.

Makes 4 chunky burgers

60ml (4 tbsp) Smoky Barbecue Sauce	125g (4oz) piece of day-old white bread (with crusts)
1 garlic clove, skinned and crushed	1 free-range egg, beaten
5ml (1 level tsp) mild mustard	seasoned flour for coating
15ml (1 tbsp) runny honey	vegetable or olive oil for frying
175g (6oz) frozen TVP mince	

1 Put the Barbecue Sauce, garlic, mustard and honey in a bowl and mix well. Add the (still frozen) mince and stir to coat in the mixture.

2 Roughly chop the bread, then put it in a food processor and process just long enough to make chunky breadcrumbs. Add the mince mixture and process again until well mixed and just starting to cling together. Tip back into the bowl and add the egg to bind.

3 Divide the mixture into four. Using floured hands, take one portion and squeeze and pat the mixture into a thick burger. You will need to be fairly firm to get it to stick together. Coat generously in seasoned flour, then repeat with the remaining mixture to make four burgers.

4 Heat a little oil in a frying pan until fairly hot. Add the burgers and cook over a high heat for about 5 minutes or until browned on the underside. Turn the burgers over and cook until the other side is browned. Serve hot in burger buns with lettuce, tomato and relishes, or serve with Honey-glazed corn on the cob (see page 94).

Calzone

This recipe makes six individual pizza turnovers. If you're short of time, make two large turnovers instead.

Serves 6

1 quantity Pizza dough (see page 88)	**15ml (1 tbsp) tomato purée**
30ml (2 tbsp) olive oil	**salt and pepper**
2 onions, skinned and sliced	**75g (3oz) Parmesan, Pecorino or vegetarian Cheddar cheese (or a mixture of these), grated**
a few pitted black or green olives, chopped (optional)	
75g (3oz) raisins or sultanas	**flour for sprinkling**
4 tomatoes, chopped	

1 Make the pizza dough following the instructions on page 88 and leave in a warm place to rise.

2 Meanwhile, heat the oil in a heavy-based saucepan, add the onions and sauté until very soft but not brown. Add the olives, if using, with the raisins or sultanas, the tomatoes and the tomato purée, and simmer gently for about 15 minutes or until the sauce is well reduced. Season to taste with salt and pepper. Cool slightly, then add the cheese.

3 Turn the risen dough on to a floured surface and divide into six equal pieces. Using a rolling pin, roll each to a rough circle measuring about 20cm (8 inches) in diameter.

4 Divide the filling mixture between the circles of dough and spread it out, leaving a good border around the edge. Brush the edges with water, then fold each in half to enclose the filling. Twist the edges of the pastry between your thumb and forefinger, pressing to seal the edges together. Sprinkle with a little flour.

5 Transfer the calzone to baking sheets and cover with clean tea-towels. Leave in a warm place for 20–30 minutes or until the dough looks puffy. Bake in the oven at 220°C (425°F) mark 7 for about 20 minutes or until well risen and golden brown. Leave to cool slightly before serving.

Pizza (page 88)

Vegetable pancakes

Pancakes are fun to make and they're quick, too – it's the filling, rolling and baking that can make them seem laborious when hungry children are waiting. So I devised this recipe for pancakes that can be eaten without any filling, simply topped with tomato sauce and grated cheese. You will notice that the list of ingredients includes a *grated* red pepper. Providing your pepper is fresh and your grater sharp, it does work! In case you do have more time (or are making pancakes in advance), I've given a few filling suggestions at the end of the recipe.

Makes about 10

50g (2oz) plain wholemeal or buckwheat flour	1 small red pepper, seeded and grated
50g (2oz) plain white flour	salt and pepper
1 free-range egg	vegetable oil for frying
about 300ml (½ pint) milk	TO SERVE
1 small courgette, trimmed and grated	tomato sauce (see pages 125–6)
1 small carrot, peeled and grated	grated vegetarian Cheddar cheese

1 Put the flours in a bowl and mix together. Make a well in the centre and add the egg. Pour in half the milk and beat with the egg in the well, gradually beating in the flour until you have a very thick batter. Pour in enough of the remaining milk, bit by bit, beating all the time, until the batter has the consistency of single cream. You may need to add a little extra milk. (Alternatively, to make the batter in a food processor, put the milk and egg in first, process to mix, then add the dry ingredients. Process for a few more seconds until smooth.)

2 Add the grated vegetables to the pancake mixture and mix thoroughly. Season.

3 Heat a little oil in an 18cm (7 inch) frying pan until hot. Swirl it round so that it coats the base and sides of the pan, then pour off any excess. Pour in about 45ml (3 tbsp) of the batter or enough to coat the base of the pan thinly. Cook for about 3 minutes or until the pancake is set and browned on the underside.

4 Turn or toss the pancake and cook the second side until golden brown. Remove from the pan and cook the remaining pancakes in the same way, adding more oil to the pan as necessary. As each pancake is cooked, either serve immediately, or pile them up, interleaved with greaseproof paper, and keep them warm in the oven until they are all cooked. (If you intend filling them, it is not necessary to keep them warm, as they will be warmed through once filled.)

5 Serve the hot pancakes plain, or spread them with tomato sauce and sprinkle with grated vegetarian Cheddar cheese.

PANCAKE FILLINGS

Cottage Cheese Top each pancake with plain cottage cheese or with cottage cheese flavoured with chopped spring onions. Roll up the pancakes and place in an oven-proof dish. Sprinkle with grated cheese and breadcrumbs and bake in the oven at 180°C (350°F) mark 4 for about 20 minutes or until golden brown.

Bean and Ratatouille Mix about 125g (4oz) cooked beans with 1 quantity Ratatouille (see page 92). Use to fill the pancakes and bake as for Cottage Cheese pancakes.

Mushroom Sauté mushrooms with garlic in a little oil. Use to fill the pancakes and bake as for Cottage Cheese pancakes.

Aubergine and bean gratin

Vegans could sprinkle these stuffed aubergines with a mixture of breadcrumbs, ground almonds and sesame seeds, instead of Parmesan cheese.

Serves 4

2 aubergines	225g (8oz) soaked and cooked dried cannellini beans (see page 12) or one 425g (15oz) can of cannellini beans, drained and rinsed
30ml (2 tbsp) olive oil	
1 onion, skinned and chopped	
1 garlic clove, skinned and crushed	2 tomatoes, chopped
	pepper
125g (4oz) button mushrooms, wiped and halved	30ml (2 level tbsp) freshly grated Parmesan cheese

1 Cut the ends off the aubergines and cook the aubergines in boiling water for about 10 minutes or until tender.
2 Drain the aubergines, cut in half lengthways and scoop out the flesh, leaving a 0.5cm (¼ inch) shell. Finely chop the flesh and reserve the shells.
3 Heat the oil in a frying pan, add the onion, garlic and chopped aubergine flesh, and cook gently for 5 minutes. Add the mushrooms, beans, tomatoes and pepper to taste. Cook for a further 5 minutes or until the mushrooms are cooked.
4 Stuff the aubergine shells with the chopped aubergine mixture and sprinkle with Parmesan cheese. Cook under a grill for 4–5 minutes or until heated through.

NUTRITION

Good source of

F   VC

Spinach tortilla

A tortilla makes a filling main course and is amazingly versatile; vary the basic potato and onion mixture to suit your family's likes and dislikes (mushrooms or courgettes are good). Wrap any leftover tortilla, chill and serve it cold for lunch or as part of a packed lunch the following day.

Serves 6–8

450g (1lb) waxy potatoes (such as Wilja or Maris Bard)	**1 garlic clove, skinned and crushed (optional)**
salt and pepper	**a large handful of fresh spinach, washed and trimmed**
about 60ml (4 tbsp) olive oil	
2 onions, skinned and chopped	**6 free-range eggs**

1 Put the potatoes in a pan of cold water with a pinch of salt and bring to the boil. Lower the heat and simmer for 5 minutes. Drain and leave until cool enough to handle, then peel off the skins (or leave them on if you prefer) and slice the potatoes thickly.

2 Heat half the oil in a large, heavy-based, preferably non-stick, frying pan. Add the potatoes, onions and garlic, and cook over a fairly high heat for a few minutes to brown the potatoes. Lower the heat and cook for a further 5 minutes or until the potatoes are very soft.

3 Tear the spinach into small pieces and sprinkle over the potato mixture with salt and pepper to taste. Stir until the spinach is just wilted. Loosen any sediment from the bottom of the pan, then pat the ingredients into an even layer with the back of a wooden spoon.

4 Beat together the eggs, then pour into the pan. Cook over a high heat for a few minutes or until the egg looks set around the edges. Loosen the tortilla from the sides of the pan and shake it to make sure that it is loose underneath. Put a large plate upside down on top of the pan, then quickly invert the pan and the plate to turn the tortilla out on to the plate.

5 Heat the remaining oil in the pan, then slide the tortilla back into the pan, browned side up. Cook over a high heat until the tortilla is cooked on the underside. Turn out and serve hot or cold, cut into wedges like a cake.

Aduki and haricot bean casserole

Serve this casserole with a grain such as rice, barley or wheat.

Serves 6

75g (3oz) dried aduki beans, soaked overnight in cold water and drained	1 large courgette, trimmed and sliced
125g (4oz) dried haricot beans, soaked overnight in cold water and drained	125g (4oz) mushrooms, wiped and sliced
30ml (2 tbsp) vegetable oil	125g (4oz) runner beans, cut into 2.5cm (1 inch) pieces
½ Spanish onion, skinned and finely chopped	400g (14oz) can of chopped tomatoes
2 garlic cloves, skinned and crushed	30ml (2 level tbsp) chopped fresh basil or 15ml (1 level tbsp) dried
1 celery stick, trimmed and chopped	30ml (2 level tbsp) chopped fresh oregano or marjoram or 15ml (1 level tbsp) dried oregano
1 carrot, peeled and chopped	15ml (1 level tbsp) chopped fresh parsley
2 potatoes, scrubbed and cut into large chunks	freshly grated Parmesan cheese, to serve (optional)
900ml (1½ pints) vegetable stock	

1 Put the beans in two separate saucepans and cover with fresh water. Bring to the boil and boil for 10–15 minutes, then drain and rinse.

2 Put the haricot beans back in the saucepan, cover with fresh water and bring to the boil, then lower the heat and simmer for 1¼ hours or until tender. Cook the aduki beans in a separate pan of fresh water for 30 minutes or until tender. Drain and rinse both lots of beans.

3 Heat the oil in a large saucepan, add the onion and cook for 5 minutes or until soft.

Add the garlic and cook for a further 2 minutes, then add the celery, carrot and potatoes. Stir until coated with the oil, then add the haricot and aduki beans, and the vegetable stock. Cook, half covered, for 15 minutes.

4 Add the courgette, mushrooms and runner beans and continue cooking for 5 minutes. Stir in the tomatoes, basil, oregano or marjoram and parsley, and cook for 5 minutes longer. Serve sprinkled with a little Parmesan cheese, if liked.

NUTRITION

Good source of

(F) (VA) (VC)

Bean, potato and leek pie

Before rolling out the pastry, check that your baking sheet is large enough. If not, make the pie shorter and squarer to fit. Any leftover pie can be eaten cold or reheated.

Serves 8

450g (1lb) floury potatoes (such as King Edward or Maris Piper), peeled and roughly chopped	150g (5oz) full-fat soft cheese
salt and pepper	225g (8oz) soaked and cooked black-eyed beans (see page 12) or one 425g (15oz) can of black-eyed beans, drained and rinsed
30ml (2 tbsp) vegetable oil	
1 large onion, skinned and chopped	freshly grated nutmeg
450g (1lb) leeks, trimmed, washed and sliced	two 370g (13oz) packets of frozen puff pastry, thawed
225g (8oz) mushrooms, wiped and sliced	water, milk or beaten free-range egg, to glaze
125g (4oz) fresh spinach, trimmed and washed	sesame seeds

1 Cook the potatoes in boiling, salted water for 10–15 minutes or until tender. Drain well and leave to cool.

2 Meanwhile, heat the oil in a large saucepan, add the onion and leeks, and fry for 5–10 minutes or until soft. Add the mushrooms and continue cooking until the mushrooms are soft. Add the spinach and cook for 1 minute or until the spinach has just wilted. Add the full-fat soft cheese, the beans and potatoes, and season generously with salt, pepper and nutmeg. Cool.

3 Thinly roll out one packet of pastry on a lightly floured surface to a rectangle measuring about 33cm (13 inches) long and 25.5cm (10 inches) wide. Transfer the pastry to a baking sheet.

4 Spoon the filling on to the pastry, leaving a 2.5cm (1 inch) border around the edge. Roll out the second piece of pastry and use to cover the first. Brush the edges with water, milk or beaten egg and press together to seal. Lightly mark squares on the pastry with the back of a knife. Brush with milk or beaten egg and sprinkle with sesame seeds. Bake in the oven at 200°C (400°F) mark 6 for 30–35 minutes or until well risen and golden brown.

NUTRITION

Good source of

C   F   P

Bean and parsnip pie

To make this pie suitable for vegans, use vegan cheese or omit the cheese altogether and bind the filling with hummus.

Serves 6–8

30ml (2 tbsp) vegetable oil	30ml (2 tbsp) crème fraîche, mascarpone cheese or soured cream
1 onion, skinned and chopped	salt and pepper
225g (8oz) parsnips, peeled and roughly chopped	two 225g (8oz) packets of puff pastry, thawed if frozen
2 carrots, peeled and grated	175g (6oz) vegetarian Cheddar cheese, grated
1 cooking apple, peeled, cored and grated	2 spring onions, chopped
125g (4oz) soaked and cooked dried beans of your choice (see page 12), or half a 425g (15oz) can of beans, drained and rinsed	free-range beaten egg or milk for brushing
	freshly grated Parmesan cheese (optional)

1 Heat the oil in a frying pan, add the onion and cook for about 5 minutes or until softened. Add the parsnips, carrots and apple, and continue cooking for a few minutes, stirring all the time.

2 Add 150ml (¼ pint) water and bring to the boil, then lower the heat and cover the pan with a lid or a piece of foil. Simmer for about 15 minutes or until the vegetables are very tender and the mixture quite dry. If it is very wet, remove the lid, increase the heat and boil rapidly to reduce. Add the beans and crème fraîche, mascarpone or soured cream, and season with salt and pepper. Leave to cool.

3 Meanwhile, thinly roll out one of the packets of pastry on a lightly floured surface.

Sprinkle with half the cheese and spring onions. Fold the pastry in half to enclose the cheese and onions, press to seal, then roll out again to a 25.5cm (10 inch) circle. Repeat with the second packet of pastry.

4 Place one sheet of pastry on a dampened baking sheet and spoon the filling into the middle, leaving a 5cm (2 inch) border around the edge. Brush the edge with egg or milk, then put the second sheet of pastry on top. Press the edges together to seal. Make a series of cuts around the edge of the pastry, brush with more egg or milk and sprinkle with Parmesan, if using.

5 Bake the pie in the oven at 200°C (400°F) mark 6 for 25–30 minutes or until well risen and golden brown.

NUTRITION

Good source of

P   **C**

Bean and ratatouille pie

If you have time, you could reserve a little of the pastry and cut out a few shapes – which need not be leaves, but something in keeping with the latest kids' craze, dinosaurs for example. Stick these to the pastry edge with a little beaten egg, milk or water. This pie could also be made with any of the other pastries on pages 120–21 and the cheese is entirely optional if you would like to make a vegan pie.

Serves 8

1½ quantities Cheese pastry (see page 120)	beaten free-range egg or milk, to glaze
1 quantity Ratatouille (see page 92)	about 50g (2oz) vegetarian Cheddar cheese, grated (optional)
225g (8oz) soaked and cooked dried beans of your choice (see page 12), or one 425g (15oz) can of beans, drained and rinsed	

1 Roll out the pastry on a lightly floured surface to a 35.5cm (14 inch) circle and use to line a 23cm (9 inch) loose-bottomed flan tin. Press the pastry over the base and into the sides, but do not trim away the edges (they should hang over the sides of the tin). Stand the tin on a baking sheet.

2 Mix together the ratatouille and the beans, and spoon into the pastry case. Fold the excess pastry over the filling. Brush with egg or milk and sprinkle with cheese, if using.

3 Bake the pie in the oven at 200°C (400°F) mark 6 for 30–35 minutes or until well browned. Serve warm.

NUTRITION

Good source of

C   VA   VC

Vegetable couscous

For a more elaborate dish, stir a few toasted flaked almonds and a handful of chopped coriander into the cooked couscous grains.

Serves 6

125g (4oz) chick peas, soaked overnight in cold water	1.25ml (¼ level tsp) chilli powder
225g (8oz) couscous	2 leeks, trimmed and sliced
15ml (1 tbsp) vegetable oil	2 carrots, peeled and sliced
2 onions, skinned and chopped	600ml (1 pint) vegetable stock
1 garlic clove, skinned and crushed	3 courgettes, trimmed and sliced
5ml (1 level tsp) ground cumin	1 large tomato, coarsely chopped
5ml (1 level tsp) ground coriander	50g (2oz) raisins
	50g (2oz) no-need-to-soak dried apricots

1 Drain the chick peas, put them in a saucepan and cover with fresh water. Bring to the boil and boil rapidly for 10–15 minutes. Lower the heat and simmer for 40–50 minutes, then drain.

2 Meanwhile, put the couscous in a bowl and add 450ml (¾ pint) cold water. Leave to soak for 10–15 minutes or until the water has been absorbed.

3 Heat the oil in a large saucepan, add the onions and cook for 5 minutes. Add the garlic and spices and cook, stirring, for 1 minute. Add the leeks, carrots and stock. Bring to the boil.

4 Line a large sieve with muslin or a clean J-cloth and place over the vegetable stew. Put the couscous in the sieve. Cover the whole pan with foil to enclose the steam, and simmer the stew for 20 minutes.

5 Add the chick peas, courgettes, tomato, raisins and apricots to the stew. Replace the sieve and fluff up the couscous with a fork. Cover and simmer for 10 minutes. Serve the stew with the couscous.

NUTRITION

Good source of

F I VA VC

Spinakopitta

Look out for time-saving bags of ready-prepared spinach in the shops. This pie may be served hot, or eaten cold as part of a lunchbox.

Serves 8

15ml (1 tbsp) olive oil	freshly grated nutmeg, to taste
1 onion, skinned and chopped	salt and pepper
1–2 garlic cloves, skinned and crushed	125g (4oz) feta cheese, crumbled
2.5ml (½ level tsp) ground cinnamon	125g (4oz) cottage cheese
1.4kg (3lb) fresh spinach, washed, trimmed and roughly chopped or three 225g (8oz) packets of frozen spinach	30ml (2 level tbsp) freshly grated Parmesan cheese
	1 egg, beaten
15ml (1 level tbsp) chopped fresh oregano or marjoram or 7.5ml (1½ level tsp) dried	225g (8oz) filo pastry, thawed if frozen

1 Lightly grease a 25cm (10 inch) shallow, round baking dish and set aside. Heat the olive oil in a large saucepan, add the onion and garlic, and cook for 5 minutes or until softened, stirring frequently. Stir in the cinnamon and cook for 1 minute, stirring constantly.

2 Add the spinach. Cook with just the water clinging to the leaves for about 5 minutes or until wilted, stirring frequently, or cook for 10 minutes if using frozen spinach.

3 Stir in the herbs and nutmeg, and season with salt and pepper. Cook for 3–4 minutes or until the moisture evaporates. Stir in the cheeses and the egg, and mix thoroughly. Set aside.

4 Use half of the pastry to line the baking dish, cutting it so that it overlaps the dish by about 5cm (2 inches) all the way round.

5 Spoon in the filling and level the surface. Bring the overlapped pastry up over the filling. Cut the remaining pastry in half and place on top of the pie, one piece on top of the other, tucking under the edges to enclose the filling completely.

6 Brush the pie with a little olive oil, score the top into squares and cook at 180°C (350°F) mark 4 for about 45 minutes or until golden brown. Serve hot or cold.

NUTRITION

Good source of

C   I   VB$_2$ VA   VC   FA

Baked jacket potatoes

Baked jacket potatoes make a filling, inexpensive meal that needs little or no accompaniment. Serve the potatoes split and topped with one of the following: a knob of vegetable margarine or butter and a handful of grated vegetarian Cheddar; a dollop of cottage cheese or yogurt; sweetcorn mixed with a little fromage frais; Guacamole (see page 36); Creamy hummus (see page 33); Ratatouille (see page 92). Alternatively, try one of the fillings suggested below.

Serves 4–8

4 potatoes, about 175g (6oz) each	CHILLI BEAN FILLING
vegetable oil (optional)	400g (14oz) can of chopped tomatoes
CARROT, PEANUT AND ALFALFA FILLING	10ml (2 level tsp) tomato purée
75ml (5 tbsp) natural yogurt	2 garlic cloves, skinned and crushed
45ml (3 tbsp) peanut butter	2.5ml (½ level tsp) chilli powder
45ml (3 tbsp) mayonnaise	2.5ml (½ level tsp) dried oregano
4 large carrots, peeled and coarsely grated	425g (15oz) soaked and cooked red kidney beans (see page 12) or one 425g (15oz) can of red kidney beans, drained and rinsed
75g (3oz) roasted peanuts	
75g (3oz) alfalfa sprouts	
a squeeze of lemon juice	30ml (2 level tbsp) chopped fresh coriander or parsley
pepper	salt and pepper

1 Wash and scrub the potatoes and prick all over with a fork. If you prefer baked potatoes with softish skins, rub the potatoes all over with a little oil; for very crunchy skins, put them into the oven while still wet.

2 Bake the potatoes in the oven at 230°C (450°F) mark 8 for about 1 hour or at 200°C (400°F) mark 6 for about 1½ hours or until the potatoes feel soft when gently squeezed, turning them over once during cooking. (They can be cooked at a lower temperature if, for example, you are cooking a casserole in the oven at the same time, but of course they will take much longer.)

3 While the potatoes are cooking, make the required filling (see opposite).

4 When the potatoes are cooked, cut them in half and mash the flesh lightly with a fork. Pile the prepared filling on top and serve immediately.

FILLINGS

Carrot, Peanut and Alfalfa Beat the yogurt, peanut butter and mayonnaise together, then gradually fold in the carrots, peanuts and alfalfa. Season with lemon juice and pepper, and use to fill the potatoes.

Chilli Bean Put all the ingredients into a saucepan, season with salt and pepper, and bring to the boil. Cook vigorously for 15–20 minutes or until reduced and thickened. Use to fill the potatoes.

Gnocchi

The soft, unchallenging texture of these little Italian 'dumplings' makes them suitable for very young children. Use a variety of canned tomatoes without extra juice or they will make the finished dish too wet.

Serves 6

175g (6oz) semolina
900ml (1½ pints) milk
salt and pepper
1 free-range egg
125g (4oz) mature vegetarian Cheddar cheese, grated

400g (14oz) can of chopped tomatoes
25g (1oz) butter
freshly grated Parmesan cheese or extra grated vegetarian Cheddar cheese for sprinkling

1 Put the semolina and milk in a non-stick saucepan and bring to the boil, stirring all the time. Cook over a high heat for about 3 minutes or until very thick. Remove from the heat and season with salt and pepper. Add the egg and cheese, mix thoroughly and leave to cool.

2 Pour the tomatoes into a shallow heatproof dish. Spread them out so that they make a thin layer in the base of the dish. Season with a little salt and pepper.

3 Shape the gnocchi mixture into small balls and arrange in a single layer on top of the tomatoes. Dot with butter and sprinkle generously with cheese. Cook under a hot grill for 5–10 minutes or until the gnocchi are cooked through and the cheese has melted and is golden brown and bubbling.

NUTRITION

Good source of

VA   **VC**

Shepherdess pie

This is a vegetarian version of the popular family dish. Instead of the lentil mixture, you could use 1 quantity Bolognese sauce (see page 123). A generous handful of grated cheese, sprinkled over the potato before baking, is a good addition. For a vegan dish, mash the potatoes with olive oil.

Serves 6

30ml (2 tbsp) olive oil	300ml (½ pint) vegetable stock
1 aubergine, trimmed and chopped	salt and pepper
125g (4oz) mushrooms, wiped and sliced	900g (2lb) potatoes, peeled and halved
1 garlic clove, skinned and crushed	45ml (3 tbsp) milk
175g (6oz) split red lentils	40g (1½oz) vegetable margarine or butter
1 bouquet garni	

1 Heat the oil in a heavy-based saucepan, add the aubergine, mushrooms and garlic, and cook over a high heat until slightly browned. Add the lentils, bouquet garni and stock, and season with salt and pepper.
2 Bring the mixture to the boil, then lower the heat, half cover the pan with a lid and simmer for about 20 minutes or until the lentils are reduced to a mush. If the mixture is very wet, boil rapidly to reduce.
3 Meanwhile, cook the potatoes in boiling salted water for about 20 minutes or until tender. Drain and mash with the milk and half the margarine or butter.
4 Remove the bouquet garni from the lentil mixture and spoon the mixture into an ovenproof dish. Cover with the mashed potato. Swirl the top with a fork and dot with the remaining margarine or butter. Bake in the oven at 200°C (400°F) mark 6 for about 20 minutes or until golden brown. Cool slightly before serving.

NUTRITION

Good source of

C

Macaroni cheese

This makes a fairly large amount (in children's terms), but it is a good idea to make a lot and freeze the extra in portion sizes ready for reheating in the microwave.
Serve with halved cherry tomatoes, or steamed or boiled carrots, peas, beans or courgettes.

Serves 8

225g (8oz) short-cut macaroni or small pasta shapes	**a pinch of freshly grated nutmeg or 2.5ml (½ level tsp) prepared mustard (optional)**
salt and pepper	**225g (8oz) mature vegetarian Cheddar cheese, grated**
65g (2½oz) vegetable margarine or butter	**45ml (3 level tbsp) fresh wholemeal breadcrumbs**
65g (2½oz) plain flour	
900ml (1½ pints) full-fat milk	

1 Cook the macaroni in boiling salted water for about 10 minutes or until just tender. Drain well.

2 Meanwhile, melt the margarine or butter in a saucepan, stir in the flour and cook gently for 1 minute. Remove the pan from the heat and gradually stir in the milk. Bring to the boil and continue to cook, stirring, until the sauce thickens, then remove from the heat, season with salt and pepper and add the nutmeg or mustard, if using, most of the cheese and the macaroni.

3 Pour into an ovenproof dish and sprinkle with the remaining cheese and the breadcrumbs.

4 Brown under a hot grill or place on a baking sheet and bake in the oven at 200°C (400°F) mark 6 for 25–30 minutes or until golden and bubbling.

NUTRITION

Good source of

C   P

VARIATION

Cauliflower Cheese Omit the macaroni. Trim 1 large cauliflower and cut into very small florets (you will need about 800g/1¾lb florets). Cook the florets in fast boiling salted water for about 10 minutes or until just tender, then drain. For very young children, chop the florets into tiny pieces. Place in an ovenproof dish. Make the sauce and pour over the cauliflower. Sprinkle with the remaining cheese and breadcrumbs and brown under a hot grill or bake in the oven as for Macaroni cheese.

Barbecue tofu kebabs

You could add any other vegetables you like to these quickly made kebabs. Serve in pitta bread or with Stir-fried vegetables (see page 84).

Makes 12 kebabs

30ml (2 tbsp) light soy sauce	2 garlic cloves, skinned and crushed
30ml (2 tbsp) tomato purée	
30ml (2 tbsp) brown sugar	300g (10oz) packet of firm tofu
15ml (1 tbsp) wine vinegar	
15ml (1 tbsp) sesame, peanut or vegetable oil	2 courgettes, trimmed and thickly sliced, or a few baby corn cobs

1 Mix together the first six ingredients. Cut the tofu into small bite-sized cubes and mix with the sauce. Thread the tofu and vegetables on to wooden skewers.

2 Cook the kebabs under a hot grill, turning frequently and brushing with the sauce, until browned on all sides and the vegetables are cooked.

Left to right: Barbecue tofu kebabs (above),
Stir-fried vegetables (page 84)

Stir-fried vegetables

Vegetable stir-fries are delicious made with whatever vegetables you have to hand, though it's important to cut them all into pieces of a similar size. Add tougher, slower-cooking vegetables, such as baby corn cobs, carrots, green beans, onions, peppers and celery, first. Delicate fast-cooking vegetables, such as bean sprouts, Chinese leaves, pak choi and spinach, need only 2–3 minutes in the hot oil. If you are preparing this dish for very young children, finely chop the nuts before returning them to the vegetables.

Serves 4–6

60ml (4 tbsp) vegetable oil	900g (2lb) mixed vegetables, prepared as necessary and cut into thin strips or slices
2 garlic cloves, skinned and crushed	15ml (1 tbsp) light soy sauce
125g (4oz) cashew nuts, peanuts or almonds	15ml (1 tbsp) dry sherry (optional)
	5ml (1 level tsp) sugar

1 Heat the oil in a wok or very large, deep frying pan. Add the garlic and stir-fry for 1–2 minutes. Add the nuts and cook for 2 minutes, stirring all the time. Remove the pan from the heat, remove the nuts with a slotted spoon and set aside.

2 Reheat the oil, then sprinkle in any slow-cooking vegetables. Cook over a very high heat for 3–4 minutes, stirring all the time. Add the remaining vegetables and cook for a further 2–3 minutes or until heated through but still very crisp.

3 Add the soy sauce, sherry, if using, and sugar. Cook for a further 1 minute, then transfer to a warmed serving dish, sprinkle with the nuts and serve immediately.

NUTRITION

Good source of

VC

VARIATIONS

Stir-fried Vegetables with Coconut Milk
Omit the nuts, soy sauce, sherry and sugar. Dissolve 175g (6oz) creamed coconut in 450ml (¾ pint) boiling water. Mix with 5ml (1 level tsp) ground cumin and 30ml (2 level tbsp) chopped fresh coriander.

Cook the vegetables as above, then remove them from the pan and set aside. Add the coconut mixture to the hot oil and cook for 1 minute, stirring all the time. Return the vegetables to the pan and reheat for 1–2 minutes.

Stir-fried Vegetables with Tofu or Quorn Marinate 225g (8oz) diced tofu or Quorn in 30ml (2 tbsp) soy sauce and 30ml (2 tbsp) dry sherry with 1 skinned and crushed garlic clove for at least 30 minutes before cooking. Drain the Quorn or tofu and stir-fry in hot oil for 2–3 minutes.

Remove from the pan and set aside. Cook the vegetables and add the soy sauce mixture as in the main recipe, or add the coconut mixture, as in Stir-fried Vegetables with Coconut Milk. Stir in the Quorn or tofu at the end and reheat for 1–2 minutes before serving.

Vegetable loaf

Serve this loaf hot with Tomato sauce (see pages 125–6) or Cheese sauce (see page 121) and a crisp salad.

Serves 6

10ml (2 tsp) vegetable oil	75g (3oz) vegetarian Cheddar cheese, grated
350g (12oz) carrots, peeled and grated	3 large free-range eggs (size 2), beaten
350g (12oz) courgettes, trimmed and grated	45ml (3 tbsp) low-fat natural yogurt
225g (8oz) leeks, trimmed and finely shredded	30ml (2 level tbsp) chopped fresh parsley
1 garlic clove, skinned and crushed	salt and pepper
150g (5oz) fresh wholemeal breadcrumbs	

1 Lightly grease a 1.2 litre (2 pint) loaf tin and line the base with greased greaseproof paper. Heat the oil in a saucepan, add the vegetables and garlic, and cook gently for 5 minutes. Drain off the liquid and mix the vegetables with the breadcrumbs, cheese, eggs, yogurt and parsley. Season with salt and pepper.

2 Transfer the mixture to the prepared loaf tin and cover with greased foil. Stand the loaf tin in a roasting tin and add enough hot water to come halfway up the sides of the loaf tin. Bake in the oven at 180°C (350°F) mark 4 for 55–60 minutes or until set.

3 Ease the cooked loaf away from the tin with a palette knife and invert on to a serving dish. Cut into slices to serve.

NUTRITION

Good source of

VA   VC

Cauliflower cheese tart

This can also be served cold and is useful for including in a lunchbox.

Serves 8

225g (8oz) Shortcrust pastry or one of the variations given on pages 120–21	2 free-range eggs
350g (12oz) cauliflower florets	150g (5oz) vegetarian Cheddar cheese, grated
salt and pepper	45ml (3 tbsp) fresh breadcrumbs
300ml (½ pint) Greek-style yogurt	

1 Roll out the pastry on a lightly floured surface and use to line a 23cm (9 inch) fluted flan dish. Bake blind in the oven at 200°C (400°F) mark 6 for 10 minutes. Remove the paper and baking beans and bake for a further 5 minutes or until the pastry case is just cooked. Remove from the oven and turn the oven temperature down to 180°C (350°F) mark 4.

2 Cook the cauliflower in boiling salted water for 5 minutes or until softened but still with some 'bite'. Drain thoroughly.

3 Beat together the yogurt, eggs and half the cheese, and season with salt and pepper. Arrange the cauliflower in the pastry case, then pour over the yogurt mixture. Sprinkle with the remaining cheese and the breadcrumbs. Bake in the oven for about 25 minutes or until set and golden brown. Serve warm.

NUTRITION

Good source of

VC

Pizza

This basic pizza dough can be rolled out to almost any size or shape you fancy, but, as a rough guide, it will make one large rectangular pizza measuring about 38 x 30.5cm (15 x 12 inches), two 30.5cm (12 inch) round pizzas or four thin 20cm (8 inch) round pizzas. Be guided by the size of your baking equipment – special round pizza pans are available but not essential. A very large, flat baking sheet, or even a large roasting tin, works just as well. Packet bread mix also makes a good quick base. You will need two 284g (10oz) packets (or the equivalent) to make the same quantity. When making up the mix, substitute 30ml (2 tbsp) olive oil for some of the liquid.

When it comes to toppings for pizza, it is difficult, and unnecessary, to suggest exact quantities since it depends on the size of the pizza(s) made and your personal taste. Whichever combinations you choose, be generous! In addition to the toppings, sprinkle thinly sliced garlic, fresh or dried herbs (such as oregano, marjoram or basil), capers or olives on to the pizza for extra flavour. As well as these adult-style toppings, some children like all manner of strange and wholly unauthentic ingredients on a pizza – sweetcorn kernels or baby corn cobs (blanch them first), pineapple chunks, sultanas or raisins, peas and even baby carrots. As long as they enjoy it, don't worry about mismatched combinations.

Serves 4

450g (1lb) strong white or wholemeal flour	**olive oil**
5ml (1 level tsp) fast-action dried yeast	**three 400g (14oz) cans of chopped tomatoes**
salt and pepper	

1 Put the flour, yeast and 5ml (1 level tsp) salt in a bowl and mix together. Make a well in the centre and add 300ml (½ pint) tepid water with 30ml (2 tbsp) olive oil. Beat thoroughly with your hand until the dough leaves the sides of the bowl clean. You may need to add more tepid water, particularly if using wholemeal flour.

2 Turn the dough on to a lightly floured surface and knead for about 10 minutes or until smooth and elastic. Roll out to the size and shape of your choice and place on a baking sheet(s). Spread with the tomatoes and add the topping(s) of your choice (see opposite). Season with salt and pepper and drizzle over a little olive oil. Leave in a warm place for 20–30 minutes or until the dough looks puffy around the edges.

3 Bake in the oven at 220°C (425°F) mark 7 for 20–30 minutes (depending on size) or until golden brown and bubbling. Serve the pizza hot.

TOPPINGS

Roasted Pepper Roast four large peppers under a hot grill until the skins blacken. Leave to cool, then remove the skins and seeds, and cut the flesh into strips. Scatter over the pizza(s) before cooking.

Mushroom Thinly slice some mushrooms. Fry in olive oil with a little garlic, then drain well. Scatter over the pizza(s) before cooking.

Cheese Most firm cheeses with good melting properties are suitable for topping pizzas.

Vegetable Almost any vegetable is good on a pizza: steamed fresh spinach (or well drained frozen leaf spinach); aubergine, courgettes or baby onions, cut into chunks or sliced and sautéed in olive oil; fresh tomatoes, sliced.

EXTRAS

Try adding the following to any of the above suggested toppings.

Tofu or Quorn Scatter cubes of plain or smoked tofu, or cubes of Quorn, over pizzas before baking.

Nuts (finely chopped for young children) Macadamia, pine nuts or hazelnuts are particularly good on a pizza.

Whole Cherry Tomatoes Scatter over pizzas, just before baking.

Free-Range Eggs Crack an egg on to each pizza just before baking.

Beans Cooked or drained canned beans of any variety are a good addition.

Quick pizza base

This makes the same quantity as the recipe opposite. It's much quicker to make and older children can mix it themselves, but it's not as tasty or as much fun to make as the real thing.

450g (1lb) self-raising white flour	125g (4oz) vegetable margarine or butter
5ml (1 level tsp) salt	300ml (½ pint) milk

Sift the flour and salt into a bowl, then rub in the margarine or butter until the mixture resembles fine breadcrumbs. Add the milk and mix to a soft dough. Turn out on to a lightly floured surface and knead until smooth. Roll out the dough and use as described in the Pizza recipe opposite.

Spinach and ricotta cannelloni

It's much easier to make cannelloni using sheets of lasagne than it is to make it with cannelloni tubes. If you cannot buy sheets of fresh lasagne, use dried, but cook them first according to packet instructions and reduce the final cooking time given below to about 20 minutes.

Serves 6–9

60ml (4 tbsp) olive oil	salt and pepper
2 small onions, skinned and finely chopped	1 garlic clove, skinned and crushed
30ml (2 level tbsp) tomato purée	450g (1lb) frozen leaf spinach, thawed and drained
5ml (1 level tsp) mild paprika	450g (1lb) ricotta cheese
two 400g (14oz) cans of chopped tomatoes	freshly grated nutmeg
a pinch of dried oregano	18 small sheets of fresh lasagne
300ml (½ pint) dry red wine or vegetable stock	freshly grated Parmesan cheese or breadcrumbs for sprinkling
a large pinch of sugar	

1 To make the sauce, heat half the oil in a heavy-based saucepan, add half the onion and fry for 5–10 minutes or until very soft. Add the tomato purée and paprika and fry for 2–3 minutes. Add the tomatoes, oregano, red wine or stock and sugar, and season with salt and pepper. Simmer for 20 minutes.

2 Heat the remaining oil in a large saucepan, add the garlic and remaining onion and cook for 5 minutes, stirring all the time. Add the spinach and cook for 2 minutes. Cool slightly, then add the ricotta cheese. Season with nutmeg, salt and pepper.

3 Lay the lasagne sheets on a work surface and divide the spinach mixture between them. Roll up the sheets to enclose the filling and arrange, seam-side down in a single layer, in a greased ovenproof dish. Pour the sauce over and sprinkle with Parmesan cheese or breadcrumbs. Bake in the oven at 200°C (400°F) mark 6 for 30 minutes.

NUTRITION

Good source of

VC

Quorn with peanut sauce

Quorn is a synthetic meat substitute that takes only minutes to cook and retains its shape well. Some vegetarians are put off by its convincingly meaty texture and because it is not made with free-range eggs. However, it's a good vehicle for this delicious peanut sauce. Incidentally, the sauce is also good with stir-fried vegetables, burgers and baked potatoes.

Serves 6

450g (1 lb) Quorn	**75ml (5 tbsp) crunchy peanut butter**
vegetable oil for grilling	
FOR THE MARINADE	**30ml (2 tbsp) soy sauce**
1 garlic clove, skinned and crushed	**5ml (1 level tsp) brown sugar**
45ml (3 tbsp) soy sauce	**1 garlic clove, skinned and crushed**
10ml (2 level tsp) brown sugar	**a pinch of chilli powder, or to taste**
FOR THE PEANUT SAUCE	**5ml (1 level tsp) finely grated lemon rind**
50g (2oz) creamed coconut, roughly chopped	

1 To make the marinade, mix all the ingredients together with 45ml (3 tbsp) water in a large shallow dish. Add the Quorn and stir. Cover and leave to marinate in the refrigerator for 2–3 hours or overnight.

2 Meanwhile, to make the peanut sauce, pour 150ml (¼ pint) boiling water over the coconut and stir until dissolved. Add all the remaining ingredients and mix thoroughly. Cover and leave to stand.

3 Thread the Quorn on to 18 bamboo skewers and brush with a little vegetable oil. Cook under a very hot grill for 3–4 minutes or until lightly browned, turning occasionally. Serve hot with the cold peanut sauce.

NUTRITION

Good source of

P

SIDE ORDERS

Ratatouille

Serve as an accompaniment to nut roasts, burgers or baked potatoes, or as a main course with beans, rice, pasta or warm bread.

Serves 8

50ml (2 fl oz) olive oil	450g (1lb) tomatoes, skinned, seeded and roughly chopped
2 onions, skinned and thinly sliced	
1 large garlic clove, skinned and crushed	1 green pepper, seeded and roughly chopped
350g (12oz) aubergine, halved or quartered lengthways and thinly sliced	1 red pepper, seeded and roughly chopped
	30ml (2 level tbsp) tomato purée
450g (1lb) small courgettes, trimmed and thinly sliced	salt and pepper

1 Heat the oil in a large saucepan, add the onions and garlic, and fry for about 5 minutes or until soft but not brown.

2 Add the aubergine, courgettes, tomatoes, peppers and tomato purée, and season with salt and pepper. Fry for 2–3 minutes, stirring, then cover tightly and simmer for 30–40 minutes or until all the vegetables are just tender. Stir well.

3 If the vegetables produce a great deal of liquid, boil, uncovered, for 5–10 minutes or until reduced. Taste and adjust the seasoning, if necessary. Serve hot or cold.

NUTRITION

Good source of

VA   VC   F

Puréed vegetable gratin

Puréeing vegetables makes them more appealing to fussy eaters, and mashing them with fromage frais increases the protein content of the dish. This could be prepared in advance and reheated before serving.

Serves 4

350g (12oz) parsnips, peeled and roughly chopped	45ml (3 tbsp) breadcrumbs
350g (12oz) carrots, peeled and roughly chopped	25g (1oz) vegetarian Cheddar cheese, grated (optional)
salt and pepper	25g (1oz) vegetable margarine or butter
225g (8oz) fromage frais	

1 Cook the parsnips and carrots in boiling salted water for about 15 minutes or until tender. Drain, reserving the cooking liquid. Mash until smooth with 30ml (2 tbsp) of the cooking liquid using a potato masher, or purée in a food processor. Add the fromage frais and season with a little pepper.

2 Transfer the purée to a heatproof dish. Sprinkle with the breadcrumbs and cheese, if using, and dot with the margarine or butter. Cook under a hot grill for about 5 minutes or until the top is golden and bubbling.

NUTRITION

Good source of

VA   VC

Honey-glazed corn on the cob

The naturally sweet, nutty flavour of corn makes it a vegetable that is popular with most children. Wrap the ends of the hot corn on the cob with foil, or make a slit in each end and insert two wooden lolly sticks, so that the corn can be picked up and nibbled.

Serves 1

1 fresh corn on the cob	**a little crushed garlic (optional)**
15ml (1 tbsp) runny honey	
15ml (1 tbsp) olive or vegetable oil	

1 Remove the stem, leaves and silky fibres from the corn (or simply fold the leaves back, if preferred). Cook in a pan of boiling water for 10 minutes or until a kernel of corn can easily be removed from the cob with a fork.

2 Drain the corn and pat dry with absorbent kitchen paper. Whisk together the honey, oil and garlic, if using. Brush generously all over the corn. Cook under a very hot grill until browned and glazed all over, turning frequently and brushing with more glaze as it cooks. Cool for 1–2 minutes before serving.

NUTRITION

Good source of

F   VC

Lemon dal

Although I don't usually approve of using ready-mixed curry powder, for simplicity I've used it here. A good brand is essential. To make a more adventurous dish for older children, add a little grated fresh root ginger and a handful of chopped fresh coriander. For young children or babies, make the dish milder by mixing it with natural yogurt.

Serves 4–6

225g (8oz) yellow split peas, soaked overnight in cold water	1.25ml (¼ level tsp) ground turmeric
30ml (2 tbsp) vegetable oil	finely grated rind and juice of ½ lemon
10ml (2 level tsp) mild curry powder	salt and pepper
2 garlic cloves, skinned and crushed	

1 Drain the split peas. Heat the oil in a large saucepan and fry the curry powder, garlic and turmeric for 1–2 minutes, stirring all the time.

2 Add the split peas, lemon rind and lemon juice to the pan with 300ml (½ pint) water. Bring to the boil, then lower the heat, cover and simmer for about 30 minutes or until the split peas are soft and the water has been absorbed. Beat thoroughly to mash the peas, and season to taste with salt and pepper. If the mixture is too wet, cook briefly over a high heat until reduced.

Spiced corn and banana puffs

Older children will enjoy these as an accompaniment, while for younger children they can be served as a meal on their own. The curry paste is optional.

Makes about 12

125g (4oz) plain white flour	150ml (¼ pint) milk
salt and pepper	1 large, firm banana
1 free-range egg, separated	200g (7oz) can of sweetcorn kernels, drained
10ml (2 tsp) mild curry paste (optional)	vegetable oil for deep-frying

1 Put the flour in a bowl and season with salt and pepper. Make a well in the centre and add the egg yolk. Mix together the curry paste, if using, and the milk. Pour a little into the well in the centre of the flour and beat, gradually drawing in the flour. Add the remaining milk and beat thoroughly to make a smooth, thick batter.

2 Peel and finely chop the banana and stir into the batter with the sweetcorn. Whisk the egg white until stiff, then fold in.

3 Heat the oil in a deep-fat fryer to 190°C (375°F) or until a cube of stale bread dropped into the hot oil turns golden in 30 seconds. Fry heaped tablespoonfuls of the mixture for 3–4 minutes or until crisp and golden brown. Drain on crumpled absorbent kitchen paper and serve hot.

Colcannon

This traditional Irish dish is the best way I know of getting children to eat greens.

Serves 4

225g (8oz) potatoes, peeled and roughly chopped	1 leek or onion, trimmed or skinned and chopped
salt and pepper	a knob of vegetable margarine or butter
225g (8oz) cabbage, trimmed and shredded	milk to mix

1 Cook the potatoes in boiling salted water for 10 minutes. Add the cabbage and the leek or onion and cook for a further 5–10 minutes or until all the vegetables are tender.

2 Drain all the vegetables, reserving the cooking liquid. Using a potato masher, mash the vegetables together with the margarine or butter until broken down, then add enough of the cooking liquid to make a soft mash. Add a splash of milk and then mash again. Reheat, if necessary, before serving.

Barbecue beans

The cooking time for bean dishes like this can vary enormously. If using beans that have been in the cupboard for ages, then they're likely to be a little shrivelled and to take ages to cook. Once they're in the barbecue sauce they cook very slowly, so make sure the initial cooking is sufficient. Serve as a side dish with baked potatoes, burgers or veggie bangers, or as a main course with rice.

Serves 6–8

450g (1lb) cannellini beans, soaked overnight in cold water	45ml (3 tbsp) dark soy sauce
	300ml (½ pint) apple juice
30ml (2 tbsp) vegetable oil	45ml (3 tbsp) dark brown sugar
1 onion, skinned and chopped	15ml (1 level tbsp) mild mustard
2 garlic cloves, skinned and crushed	salt and pepper
400g (14oz) can of chopped tomatoes	

1 Drain the beans and put them in a large saucepan with fresh cold water to cover. Bring to the boil and boil rapidly for 10 minutes, then reduce the heat and simmer for about 1 hour or until tender.

2 Meanwhile, heat the oil in a large saucepan, add the onion and garlic, and sauté until soft. Add the tomatoes, soy sauce, apple juice, brown sugar and mustard, bring to the boil and simmer for about 10 minutes or until slightly reduced. Remove from the heat until the beans are ready.

3 Drain the beans and add to the barbecue sauce. Bring back to the boil, then lower the heat, half cover the pan with a lid and simmer for about 30 minutes. If the sauce is very runny, boil rapidly, uncovered, until reduced. Season with salt and pepper.

NUTRITION

Good source of

(P) (F) (VA) (VC) (FA)

Clockwise from top: Veggie bangers (page 55), Chunky oven chips (page 100), Barbecue beans (above)

Chunky oven chips

There's no escaping the fact that most kids love chips. Made this way, they are slightly less work and they contain less fat than when deep-fried.

Serves 3

700g (1½lb) smallish potatoes, washed	45ml (3 tbsp) olive or vegetable oil
salt	

1 Cut the potatoes in half lengthways, then cut each half lengthways into four sticks. Put them in a large saucepan of salted water, bring to the boil and boil for 5 minutes.
2 Put the oil in a roasting tin and heat in the oven at 220°C (425°F) mark 7.

3 Drain the potatoes thoroughly and tip them into the hot oil. Shake the roasting tin so the potatoes are coated on all sides with oil. Return to the oven and cook for about 30 minutes or until the 'chips' are crisp on the outside and cooked through.

Egg fried rice

Omit the nuts if you are making this for children under five.

Serves 6

150g (5oz) long-grain white rice	125g (4oz) green beans, cut into 2.5cm (1 inch) pieces, or petits pois
salt and pepper	
30ml (2 tbsp) vegetable oil	a handful of bean sprouts
1 free-range egg, beaten	10ml (2 tsp) grated fresh root ginger
2 celery sticks, trimmed and finely chopped	15ml (1 tbsp) soy sauce, or to taste
6 spring onions, trimmed and chopped	50g (2oz) unsalted cashew nuts

1 Cook the rice in boiling salted water for about 12–15 minutes or until just tender. Drain well, rinse with boiling water, fluff up with a fork and set aside. Heat the oil in a large frying pan, pour in the egg and stir for 2–3 seconds.
2 Add the rice, celery, spring onions, green beans or peas, bean sprouts, ginger, soy sauce and seasoning. Cook quickly, stirring continuously, for 3–5 minutes or until all the ingredients are heated through.
3 Sprinkle on the cashew nuts and cook for a further 2 minutes or until the vegetables are just tender. Serve hot.

Spicy pilau rice

This is good with veggie burgers or sausages, or with stuffed mushrooms.

Serves 4–6

30ml (2 tbsp) vegetable oil	salt and pepper
1 onion, skinned and finely chopped	600ml (1 pint) vegetable stock
2.5ml (½ level tsp) cumin seeds, crushed	125g (4oz) no-need-to-soak dried apricots, chopped
10ml (2 level tsp) ground turmeric	1 bay leaf
15ml (1 tbsp) lemon juice	50g (2oz) raisins
175g (6oz) long-grain brown rice	25g (1oz) flaked almonds

1 Heat the oil in a large saucepan over a low heat. Add the onion and cook for 3 minutes or until soft. Add the spices, lemon juice and rice, and season with salt and pepper. Mix together well so the rice is coated with the spices.

2 Bring the stock to the boil in another saucepan, then add immediately to the rice and mix well. Stir in the apricots and bay leaf.

3 Cover and simmer for 30 minutes or until all the liquid has been absorbed, adding the raisins about 10 minutes before the end of cooking to allow them to soften slightly and warm through. Stir in the almonds just before serving. Serve piping hot.

Sweet tomato salad

Adding a little honey to the dressing enhances the natural sweetness of the tomatoes in this salad. I sometimes serve this sprinkled with a little grated Parmesan or vegetarian Cheddar cheese.

Serves 4

2 ripe tomatoes, sliced	2 spring onions, trimmed and finely sliced
125g (4oz) cherry tomatoes, halved	a handful of raisins
10ml (2 tsp) runny honey	a handful of pine nuts, toasted
45ml (3 tbsp) olive oil	a few basil leaves, shredded (optional)
10ml (2 tsp) orange juice	
salt and pepper	

1 Arrange all the tomatoes on a plate.
2 Using a fork, whisk together the honey, oil and orange juice. Season with salt and pepper and pour over the tomatoes. Sprinkle with the remaining ingredients and serve.

NUTRITION

Good source of

VC

Fruity vegetable salad

The inclusion of fruit in a savoury salad generally makes it more appealing to children. Omit the nuts, or chop them *very* finely, if serving to very young children.

Serves 6

15ml (1 tbsp) soy sauce	1 eating apple
30ml (2 tbsp) orange juice	about ¼ small cucumber
15ml (1 tbsp) smooth peanut butter	1 large carrot, peeled
45ml (3 tbsp) vegetable oil	50g (2oz) sprouted beans of your choice or bean sprouts
4 satsumas or 2 large seedless oranges	50g (2oz) salted peanuts

1 To make the dressing, whisk together the soy sauce, orange juice, peanut butter and oil.
2 Peel the satsumas, if using, and separate into segments. If using oranges, remove all the peel and white pith, then chop into bite-sized pieces. Stir into the dressing.

3 Core and chop the apple. Finely shred the cucumber and the carrot. Mix the apple, cucumber and carrot into the dressing and orange mixture, and add the bean sprouts and peanuts. Mix everything together well and serve immediately.

NUTRITION

Good source of

VC

Cheese and grape salad

We like this tasty salad with baked potatoes topped with Creamy hummus or Tzatziki (see page 33).

Serves 4

2 thick slices of bread	5ml (1 level tsp) mild mustard
vegetable oil for frying	5ml (1 tsp) runny honey
1 garlic clove, skinned and crushed	5ml (1 level tsp) apple juice
1 Little Gem lettuce	45ml (3 tbsp) olive oil
175g (6oz) seedless grapes	salt and pepper
125g (4oz) vegetarian Cheddar cheese or feta cheese	

1 Cut the crusts off the bread and cut the bread into neat cubes. Heat some vegetable oil in a frying pan, add the garlic and bread, and fry until the bread is crisp and golden. Remove the croûtons from the pan with a slotted spoon and drain thoroughly on crumpled absorbent kitchen paper.
2 Trim the lettuce and finely shred or tear

it into small pieces. Halve the grapes and cut the cheese into small cubes. Mix together the lettuce, grapes and cheese.
3 To make the dressing, whisk together the mustard, honey, apple juice and olive oil. Season with salt and pepper. Pour over the salad and toss together. Sprinkle with the croûtons and serve immediately.

NUTRITION

Good source of

C

DESSERTS AND BAKING

Banana and chocolate cheesecake

The rather over-the-top decoration for this cheesecake is entirely optional. Alternatives to the curls are shavings of chocolate made with a sharp swivel-type potato peeler, grated chocolate or, if you think there is enough chocolate in the base for one meal, decorate the cheesecake with banana slices dipped in lemon juice.

Serves 6–8

225g (8oz) chocolate digestive biscuits, crushed	350g (12oz) cream cheese
75g (3oz) vegetable margarine or butter, melted	300ml (½ pint) soured cream
	30ml (2 tbsp) lemon juice
15ml (1 level tbsp) Gelozone (see page 12)	50g (2oz) icing sugar, sifted
3 ripe bananas	125g (4oz) milk chocolate, to decorate

1 Mix the biscuits with the melted margarine or butter. Press into the base of a 20.5cm (8 inch) loose-bottomed or spring-release cake tin. Chill for 30 minutes.

2 Put 45ml (3 tbsp) cold water in a small saucepan and sprinkle over the Gelozone. Stir until completely dissolved, then heat gently until just steaming but not boiling. Leave to cool slightly.

3 Peel and mash the bananas, then beat together with all the remaining ingredients, except the chocolate. Add the Gelozone mixture and mix thoroughly. Pour on top of the biscuit base and chill for at least 1 hour or until set.

4 To make chocolate curls for the decoration, melt the chocolate, then spread it very thinly on the underside of one or two smooth, clean baking sheets. Leave to set, then, using a very sharp, large cook's knife held at an angle of 45° to the chocolate, carefully push it over the surface to produce curls. Alternatively, if you have a clean paint-stripping tool to hand, use this to produce larger, fatter curls. Place the curls carefully on a sheet of greaseproof paper and chill until the cheesecake is ready.

5 Serve the cheesecake with the curls piled on top.

Fruit cheesecake

This dessert can be eaten by lacto-ovo-vegetarians as it contains no gelatine.

Makes 8 slices

50g (2oz) vegetable margarine or butter	700g (1½lb) ricotta cheese
25g (1oz) medium oatmeal	3 free-range eggs
75g (3oz) plain wholemeal flour	finely grated rind of 1 lemon
40g (1½oz) light muscovado sugar	75g (3oz) caster sugar
5ml (1 level tsp) ground cinnamon	60ml (4 tbsp) Greek-style yogurt
	about 450g (1lb) fresh fruit, to decorate

1 To make the base, melt the margarine or butter in a saucepan and stir in the oatmeal, flour, sugar and cinnamon. Cook gently for 1–2 minutes, stirring, until well mixed. Press into the base of an 18cm (7 inch) loose-bottomed cake tin. Bake in the oven at 180°C (350°F) mark 4 for 5 minutes.

2 Meanwhile, beat the cheese until smooth, then add the eggs, one at a time, blending in well. Add the lemon rind and sugar, and mix thoroughly.

3 Pour on to the baked base, smooth the surface and continue baking for another 20 minutes. Spoon the yogurt over the filling and bake for a further 20 minutes.

4 Cool for about 3 hours in the tin. When cold, carefully remove the cheesecake from the tin and decorate with fruit.

Banana and grape brûlée

Children will enjoy breaking through the crunchy caramel topping on these simply made desserts.

Serves 4

2 bananas	150ml (5 fl oz) Greek-style yogurt
225g (8oz) small seedless green grapes	25g (1oz) light brown soft sugar
150ml (5 fl oz) fromage frais	

1 Peel and slice the bananas, then mix with the grapes. Spoon into four ramekins.

2 Mix the fromage frais and yogurt, and spoon over the fruit. Chill for 1 hour.

3 Sprinkle the fromage frais and yogurt mixture in each dish with a little sugar, and grill until the sugar melts and caramelises. Chill again for about 30 minutes.

Apple tarts with raspberry sauce

This simple idea works equally well with firm pears. The raspberry sauce is quick and easy to make and it's great for livening up vanilla ice cream, for serving with fromage frais or yogurt, or poured over strawberries. Older children will enjoy drizzling it over the tarts themselves.

Makes 4

225g (8oz) packet of puff or flaky pastry, thawed if frozen	**caster sugar for sprinkling**
2 small red eating apples	**350g (12oz) raspberries, thawed if frozen**
juice of 1 lemon	**about 50g (2oz) icing sugar, sifted**
25g (1oz) vegetable margarine or butter, melted	

1 Roll out the pastry on a lightly floured surface until it is very thin. Using a small plate measuring about 12.5cm (5 inches) in diameter as a guide, cut out four pastry rounds and arrange on one or two damp baking sheets.

2 Core the apples. Holding each apple on its side, cut into thin rounds. Toss in a little lemon juice to prevent discolouration. Arrange the apple rounds on top of the pastry, brush generously with melted margarine or butter and sprinkle with caster sugar.

3 Bake in the oven at 220°C (425°F) mark 7 for about 20 minutes or until dark golden brown.

4 Meanwhile, make the sauce. Push the raspberries through a nylon sieve to remove the pips. Add a squeeze of lemon juice and sifted icing sugar to taste.

5 Serve the pastries warm or cold with the sauce drizzled over.

NUTRITION

Good source of

F VC

Frozen Christmas pudding

This frozen pudding is more appealing to children than a conventional steamed Christmas pudding. The chocolate chips are optional – if you prefer to leave them out, simply increase the quantity of apricots and sultanas.

Serves 10

150ml (¼ pint) orange juice	450ml (¾ pint) double cream
60ml (4 tbsp) golden syrup	75g (3oz) chocolate chips
75g (3oz) no-need-to-soak dried apricots, finely chopped	300ml (½ pint) custard (homemade or ready-made)
75g (3oz) sultanas	chocolate curls or grated chocolate, to decorate (optional)

1 Set the freezer to 'fast freeze'. Put the orange juice and golden syrup in a small saucepan and heat gently until boiling. Add the apricots and sultanas, then cool.
2 Lightly whip the cream, then add the soaked fruit, chocolate chips and custard. Pour into a 1.3 litre (2¼ pint) pudding basin, cover and freeze for 3–4 hours or until firm. (Don't forget to switch the freezer back to the normal setting once the pudding is frozen.)
3 Transfer the pudding to the refrigerator about 30 minutes before serving. Turn out and decorate with chocolate, if liked.

Chocolate and marshmallow ice cream

This sweet treat couldn't be simpler and is always popular.

Serves 4–6

125g (4oz) milk chocolate	25g (1oz) icing sugar
400g (14oz) can of condensed milk	75g (3oz) mini marshmallows
225g (8oz) full-fat soft cheese	

1 Break the chocolate into small pieces and put it in a saucepan with the condensed milk, cheese and icing sugar. Heat gently, stirring, until the chocolate has melted. Add the marshmallows, stir to mix, then remove from the heat and leave to cool.
2 Pour the ice cream mixture into a shallow freezerproof container and freeze overnight. Store in the freezer for up to 1 month; serve from frozen.

Frozen yogurt lollies

These are even more popular if the finished frozen lollies are dipped in melted chocolate, then coated with hundreds and thousands or chopped toasted nuts.

Makes 6 small lollies

300ml (½ pint) natural yogurt	a drop of vanilla essence
15ml (1 tbsp) runny honey	

Mix together the yogurt, honey and vanilla essence, and pour into about six lolly moulds. Freeze for at least 3 hours or until solid.

VARIATIONS

Strawberry or Raspberry Yogurt Lollies Omit the vanilla essence. Put the yogurt and honey in a food processor with 125g (4oz) strawberries or raspberries. Process to a purée, then sieve. Freeze as above.

Chocolate Yogurt Lollies Omit the vanilla essence. Melt 75g (3oz) milk chocolate and mix with the yogurt and honey. Pour into lolly moulds and freeze as above.

Banana tarts

These make a popular teatime treat or lunchbox dessert.

Makes 12

175g (6oz) sweet Shortcrust pastry (see page 120)	10ml (2 level tsp) cornflour
1 large banana	25g (1oz) desiccated coconut, toasted, for sprinkling
1 free-range egg	
150ml (¼ pint) fromage frais	icing sugar for dusting
45ml (3 level tbsp) sugar	

1 Grease 12 bun tins. Thinly roll out the pastry on a lightly floured surface and cut out 12 rounds using a 7.5cm (3 inch) fluted cutter. Press one into each patty tin.
2 Peel and mash the banana, then beat in the egg, fromage frais, half the sugar and the cornflour. Divide between the pastry cases. Sprinkle generously with coconut and the remaining sugar. Bake in the oven at 190°C (375°F) mark 5 for 15–20 minutes or until golden brown and firm to the touch. Carefully remove from the tins and leave to cool on a wire rack. Sprinkle with a little icing sugar.

Toffee pie

A once-in-a-while sticky, sugary treat to be served in small portions. The chocolate decoration is entirely optional – you could embellish the pie further with chocolate flake, a few strawberries, sliced pear or banana. Young children like it best sprinkled with garishly coloured hundreds and thousands!

Serves 8

175g (6oz) plain biscuits, such as Rich Tea	400g (14oz) can of condensed milk
175g (6oz) vegetable margarine or butter	225g (8oz) fromage frais
50g (2oz) light brown soft sugar	25g (1oz) milk chocolate
	25g (1oz) plain chocolate

1 To make the base, crush the biscuits in a blender or food processor, or put in a polythene bag and crush with a rolling pin. Tip into a bowl. Melt 125g (4oz) of the margarine or butter and pour into the biscuit crumbs. Mix well, then press into the base of a 20.5cm (8 inch) loose-bottomed flan tin.

2 Put the remaining margarine or butter, the sugar and condensed milk in a heavy-based saucepan and heat gently until the sugar has dissolved. Bring to the boil, stirring all the time, then reduce the heat and simmer gently for 5 minutes or until the mixture has thickened and is a creamy fudge colour.

3 Cool the mixture slightly, then add half the fromage frais and mix thoroughly together. Pour over the biscuit base and chill in the refrigerator for at least 1 hour or until set.

4 When the pie has set, swirl the remaining fromage frais over the top. Melt the chocolate in two separate heatproof bowls over pans of hot water, and drizzle over the top of the pie.

Chocolate swirl cakes

To make plain fairy cakes, simply omit the cocoa powder and milk. Add a few sultanas instead of the chocolate chips, stirring them into the mixture rather than sprinkling them on the top.

Makes 12–15

125g (4oz) self-raising white flour	**2 free-range eggs, beaten**
5ml (1 level tsp) baking powder	**30ml (2 level tbsp) cocoa powder**
125g (4oz) caster sugar	**about 15ml (1 tbsp) milk**
125g (4oz) softened vegetable margarine or butter	**a few chocolate chips (optional)**

1 Put the flour, baking powder, sugar, margarine or butter and eggs in a bowl and beat together until smooth and glossy.

2 Put about half the mixture into another bowl and sift in the cocoa. Add enough milk to make a 'dropping' consistency.

3 Line 12 or 15 bun tins with paper cases. Put a small spoonful of the plain mixture in each, then top with a spoonful of the chocolate mixture. Swirl a knife through each to give a marbled effect. Sprinkle each bun with a few chocolate chips, if using.

4 Bake the cakes in the oven at 200°C (400°F) mark 6 for about 15 minutes or until well risen and firm to the touch. Cool on a wire rack.

Eggless chocolate cake

No one will ever guess that there's anything unusual about this cake! It's really moist, chocolaty and irresistible.

Makes about 18 slices

125g (4oz) creamed coconut	**a large pinch of salt**
50g (2oz) cocoa powder	**225g (8oz) light brown soft sugar**
400g (14oz) self-raising white flour	**200ml (7 fl oz) sunflower oil**
5ml (1 level tsp) baking powder	**icing sugar for dusting (optional)**

1 Pour 650ml (22 fl oz) boiling water over the coconut and stir until it dissolves. Leave to cool.

2 Sift the cocoa powder, flour, baking powder and salt into a bowl and mix together with the sugar. Make a well in the

centre, then pour in the coconut mixture and the oil. Using a wooden spoon, beat the ingredients together thoroughly.

3 Pour the batter into an oiled and lined 1.7 litre (3 pint) loaf tin and bake in the oven at 180°C (350°F) mark 4 for 1¼ hours or until well risen and just firm to the touch. Leave to cool in the tin for 10 minutes, then turn out and leave to cool completely. Dust with a sprinkling of icing sugar, before serving, if liked.

Carrot cake

Grated carrot lends texture and sweetness to this moist cake. It also makes it intriguing to young enquiring minds – get the children to help you mix it.

Makes 8–10 slices

225g (8oz) softened vegetable margarine or butter	5ml (1 level tsp) baking powder
225g (8oz) light brown soft sugar	50g (2oz) ground almonds
4 free-range eggs, separated	350g (12oz) young carrots, peeled and grated
finely grated rind of ½ orange	150g (5oz) walnut pieces, chopped
20ml (4 tsp) lemon juice	225g (8oz) full-fat soft cheese
175g (6oz) self-raising white flour	10ml (2 tsp) runny honey

1 Grease and line a deep 20.5cm (8 inch) round cake tin.

2 Put the margarine or butter, sugar, egg yolks, orange rind, 15ml (3 tsp) of the lemon juice, the flour, baking powder and almonds in a bowl and beat together until smooth. Add the carrots and 125g (4oz) of the walnuts.

3 Whisk the egg whites until stiff, then fold into the cake mixture. Pour into the tin and hollow the centre slightly.

4 Bake the cake in the oven at 180°C (350°F) mark 4 for 1½–2 hours or until a skewer inserted in the centre comes out clean. Cover the top with foil after 1 hour if it starts to brown.

5 Leave the cake to cool slightly, then turn it out on to a wire rack and remove the lining paper. Leave to cool.

6 To make the topping, beat together the cheese, honey and remaining lemon juice, and spread over the top of the cake. Sprinkle with the remaining walnuts.

NUTRITION

Good source of

VA

Frozen berry slush

In summer, children seem to want an endless supply of frozen lollies and ice creams. This frozen water-ice closely resembles the luridly coloured frozen 'slush' that they adore. However, this contains all the vitamins of fresh fruit and no additives. When soft fruit is plentiful, it is very cheap to make.

Serves 8

700g (1½lb) fresh ripe summer fruits, such as strawberries, raspberries and blackcurrants	175g (6oz) sugar
	30ml (2 tbsp) golden syrup
	30ml (2 tbsp) orange juice

1 Set the freezer to 'fast freeze'. Purée the fruit in a food processor, then push through a sieve to remove the pips. Add the remaining ingredients with 150ml (¼ pint) warm water. Stir until the sugar has dissolved, then add a further 300ml (½ pint) cold water.

2 Pour the mixture into a shallow freezer-proof container, cover and freeze for about 2 hours or until the mixture is frozen around the edges. Turn the mixture into a bowl and mash with a fork. Return the mixture to the freezerproof container and freeze again for about 2 hours or until completely frozen. (Don't forget to switch the freezer back to normal setting once the 'slush' is frozen.)

3 Before serving, transfer the 'slush' to the refrigerator for about 30 minutes to soften, then mash again with a fork. If you forget to take it out of the freezer, tip the whole thing into a food processor and process for 1–2 minutes or until broken down but still frozen.

VARIATIONS

Frozen Orange Slush Omit the berry purée and orange juice. Replace with 450ml (¾ pint) fresh orange juice and the juice of ½ lemon.

Frozen Pear, Apple or Pineapple Slush Omit the berry purée and orange juice. Replace with 450ml (¾ pint) fresh pear, apple or pineapple juice.

Malted sultana loaf

Serve this sliced and spread with a little vegetable margarine or butter. It's also good toasted.

Makes 12 slices

45ml (3 tbsp) malt extract	225g (8oz) self-raising wholemeal flour
450g (1lb) sultanas	
125g (4oz) dark muscovado sugar	1 large free-range egg (size 2), beaten

1 Put the malt extract, sultanas and sugar in a bowl with 450ml (¾ pint) boiling water. Leave to soak for 8 hours.
2 Grease and line a 1.7 litre (3 pint) loaf tin with greased greaseproof paper. Sift the flour on to the malt and sultana mixture, then add the egg. Mix well.

3 Pour into the prepared tin and bake in the oven at 170°C (325°F) mark 3 for about 2 hours or until risen and firm. Cover with greaseproof paper for the last 30 minutes to prevent overbrowning. Cool on a wire rack, then wrap in greaseproof paper and store for 1 day.

Oat bars

Omit the nuts or chop them *very* finely for younger children.

Makes 10

75g (3oz) vegetable margarine or butter	50g (2oz) sultanas
50g (2oz) light brown soft sugar	75g (3oz) mixed nuts, coarsely chopped
45ml (3 tbsp) runny honey	25g (1oz) no-need-to-soak dried apricots, chopped
125g (4oz) porridge oats	

1 Lightly grease and base-line a shallow 18cm (7 inch) square baking tin. Melt the margarine or butter in a saucepan, add the sugar and honey, and stir until dissolved. Add the remaining ingredients and mix well.
2 Spoon the mixture into the prepared tin,

level the surface and bake in the oven at 170°C (325°F) mark 3 for 30–35 minutes or until golden brown.
3 Leave to cool for 5 minutes in the tin, then cut into 10 fingers. When cold, transfer to an airtight container.

NUTRITION

Good source of

F

Almond shortbread with redcurrants

This rather sophisticated-sounding dessert came about because we had a glut of redcurrants in our garden this summer. Having encouraged the children to pick them, they wanted to do something interesting with them – biscuits or shortbread in fun shapes fitted the bill. Taste the redcurrants as you go; our home-grown crop was very sweet, but redcurrants can be incredibly sharp.

Makes about 16

about 175g (6oz) fresh redcurrants	150g (5oz) plain white flour
30ml (2 tbsp) fruit juice, such as orange, apple or pear	45ml (3 level tbsp) ground almonds
icing sugar for sprinkling and rolling	5ml (1 tsp) almond essence
125g (4oz) vegetable margarine or butter	mascarpone or natural yogurt, to serve
50g (2oz) caster sugar, plus extra for sprinkling	

1 Remove the stalks from the redcurrants, pick over the fruit and wash thoroughly. Drain and sprinkle with the fruit juice and icing sugar to taste. Leave to stand while making the biscuits.

2 To make the biscuits, cream together the margarine or butter and 50g (2oz) caster sugar until soft. Add the flour, ground almonds and almond essence, and mix together to form a dough. Knead lightly with your fingers. If the dough is very sticky, wrap it in cling film and chill it briefly. Roll out the dough on a surface dusted with a little icing sugar, and use shaped cutters (we used stars) to stamp out about 16 biscuit shapes.

3 Transfer the biscuits to greased baking sheets and bake in the oven at 180°C (350°F) mark 4 for about 15 minutes or until just tinged with brown around the edges. Leave to cool for 10 minutes, then remove from the baking sheets and cool on wire racks. Sprinkle with a little caster sugar, if liked.

4 To serve, spoon a pile of redcurrants on to serving plates, top with mascarpone or yogurt, and let the children add one or two biscuit shapes.

Blackberry and apple crumble pies

Individual pies and tarts are always more tempting to children but of course they are more time-consuming for the cook.

Makes 6

212g (7½oz) packet of puff or flaky pastry, thawed if frozen, or 175g (6oz) sweet Shortcrust pastry (see page 120)	150g (5oz) plain flour
	65g (2½oz) vegetable margarine or butter
	40g (1½oz) ground almonds
2 eating apples	50g (2oz) caster sugar
juice of 1 lemon	icing sugar for sprinkling
175g (6oz) blackberries	

1 Grease six 10cm (4 inch) Yorkshire pudding tins. On a lightly floured surface, roll out the pastry very thinly and cut out six rounds with a 12cm (4¾ inch) plain cutter. Line the tins with the pastry rounds and prick well.

2 Peel and core the apples and chop roughly. Mix with the lemon juice and the blackberries. Divide the mixture between the pastry cases.

3 Put the flour in a bowl and rub in the margarine or butter until the mixture resembles fine breadcrumbs. Add the almonds and caster sugar. Sprinkle the crumble over the fruit, packing it down fairly firmly with your fingertips.

4 Bake the pies in the oven at 200°C (400°F) mark 6 for about 25–30 minutes or until golden brown. Remove from the tins as soon as they are cooked to prevent them sticking. Sprinkle with icing sugar and serve warm or cold.

BASIC RECIPES

Shortcrust pastry

For shortcrust pastry, the proportion of flour to fat is two to one. Therefore, for a recipe using quantities of shortcrust pastry other than 225g (8oz), simply use half the quantity of fat to the flour weight specified. This basic pastry is suitable for most pies and flans. To make a sweet pastry, add a little caster sugar.

225g (8oz) plain white flour	**125g (4oz) vegetable margarine or butter, chilled and diced**
a pinch of salt	**chilled water**

1 Put the flour and salt in a bowl. Using both hands, rub the margarine or butter lightly into the flour until the mixture resembles fine breadcrumbs.

2 Gradually add 45–60ml (3–4 tbsp) chilled water, sprinkling it evenly over the surface. (Uneven addition may cause blistering when the pastry is cooked.) Stir with a round-bladed knife until the mixture begins to stick together in large lumps.

3 With one hand, collect the dough together to form a ball. Knead lightly for a few seconds to give a firm, smooth dough. Do not overhandle the dough.

4 Alternatively, to mix the dough in a food processor, put the flour and salt in the bowl, then add the fat and process briefly until the fat is finely chopped. Add the water and process briefly again until the dough begins to come together. Tip it out and knead briefly.

5 To roll out, sprinkle a little flour on a work surface and the rolling pin (not on the pastry) and roll out the dough evenly in one direction only, turning it occasionally. The usual thickness is 0.3cm (⅛ inch). Do not pull or stretch the pastry.

6 The pastry can be baked straight away, but it is better if allowed to 'rest' for about 30 minutes in the tin or dish, covered with greaseproof paper or foil, in the refrigerator.

7 Bake in the oven at 200–220°C (400–425°F) mark 6–7 except where otherwise specified, until lightly browned (see individual recipes).

VARIATIONS

Cheese Pastry Follow the recipe and method for Shortcrust pastry using white or wholemeal flour, or half and half, but stir in 125g (4oz) finely grated vegetarian Cheddar or other hard cheese, or 45ml (3 level tbsp) freshly grated Parmesan cheese, and a pinch of mustard powder, before adding the water.

Wholemeal Pastry Follow the recipe and method for Shortcrust pastry, but replace half the flour with wholemeal flour.

Sesame Pastry Follow the recipe and method for Shortcrust pastry using white or wholemeal flour, or half and half, but stir in 40g (1½oz) toasted sesame seeds before adding the water.

Nut Pastry Follow the recipe and method for Shortcrust pastry using white or wholemeal flour, or half and half, but stir in 40g (1½oz) very finely chopped walnuts, peanuts, cashew nuts, hazelnuts or almonds before adding the water. When using salted nuts, do not add salt to the flour in step 1.

White sauce

The quantities given here make a pouring sauce suitable for serving as an accompaniment to pies, nut roasts, vegetables and pulses.

Makes 300ml (½ pint)

15g (½oz) vegetable margarine or butter	**300ml (½ pint) milk**
15g (½oz) plain white flour	**salt and pepper**

1 Put the margarine or butter, flour and milk in a heavy-based saucepan. Heat, whisking continuously, until the sauce comes to the boil and thickens.

2 Simmer very gently for a further 2–3 minutes. Season with salt and pepper.

MICROWAVE METHOD

Put all the ingredients in a large bowl and cook on HIGH for 4–5 minutes, or until thickened, whisking every minute.

VARIATIONS

Add the following to the hot sauce with the seasoning:

Cheese Sauce Add 50g (2oz) grated vegetarian Cheddar cheese and a large pinch of mustard powder.

Mushroom Sauce Add 75g (3oz) lightly cooked sliced mushrooms.

Sweet Sauce Add 15–30ml (1–2 level tbsp) caster sugar.

Onion Sauce Add 1 onion, chopped and cooked.

Béchamel sauce

Flavoured milk gives a delicate aroma to béchamel sauce. There is a long and short method. The long method is strictly for those with time on their hands, and adults, not children, waiting to be fed. This simplified version makes a splendid sauce in half the time. It's delicious served plain or with the addition of mildly flavoured ingredients such as egg or mushroom, or use it to top lasagne or cannelloni (see pages 60 and 90).

Makes about 300ml (½ pint)

300ml (½ pint) milk	15g (½oz) vegetable margarine or butter
1 slice of onion	
1 bay leaf	scant 15g (½oz) plain white flour
6 whole peppercorns	
1 blade of mace	salt and pepper

1 Pour the milk into a saucepan. Add the onion, bay leaf, peppercorns and mace, and bring to scalding point. Remove from the heat, cover and leave to infuse for 10–30 minutes. Strain.
2 Melt the margarine or butter in a saucepan. Remove from the heat and stir in the flour until evenly blended. Gradually pour on the warm milk, stirring well. Season lightly with salt and pepper.
3 Bring to the boil, stirring constantly, and simmer for 2–3 minutes.

Egg-free mayonnaise

This is not for foodies or traditionalists but it is a useful substitute for the real thing if you are feeding vegans or if you wish to reduce the number of eggs your family is eating. The basic mixture could be flavoured with garlic, herbs, curry paste, chopped spring onion or a little tomato purée. A food processor or blender is essential. The mayonnaise will keep for about a week in the fridge.

Makes about 200ml (7 fl oz)

300g (10½oz) packet of silken tofu, drained	1.25ml (¼ level tsp) pepper
	15ml (1 tbsp) white wine or garlic vinegar
5ml (1 level tsp) Dijon mustard	
	about 90ml (6 tbsp) vegetable oil
2.5ml (½ level tsp) salt	
2.5ml (½ level tsp) sugar	

1 Put all the ingredients, except the oil, in a blender or food processor, and process until the tofu is smooth.

2 If your machine has a variable control, turn it on at a slow speed, then add the oil in a slow, steady stream until you have a smooth, thick, mayonnaise-like consistency. If your machine doesn't have this facility, add a little oil at a time, processing thoroughly between each addition. Check the seasoning and add a little more salt, pepper or mustard if required.

Bolognese sauce

This is my vegetarian version of the classic pasta sauce, with apologies to the Italians! The red wine is entirely optional (increase the stock if you prefer to leave it out) but it does give a good rich flavour; don't worry about the alcoholic content as it is destroyed by cooking. Use this sauce to dress pasta, fill lasagne or as a base for shepherd's pie. It does make a large quantity but it freezes well.

Serves 8

30ml (2 tbsp) olive oil	600ml (1 pint) vegetable stock
1 celery stick, trimmed and finely chopped	1 bay leaf
2 carrots, peeled and finely chopped	1 bouquet garni
1 onion, skinned and finely chopped	5ml (1 level tsp) yeast extract
125g (4oz) mushrooms, wiped and finely chopped	5ml (1 level tsp) sugar
	salt and pepper
2 garlic cloves, skinned and crushed	freshly grated nutmeg
	1 cinnamon stick
45ml (3 level tbsp) tomato purée	175g (6oz) textured vegetable protein (TVP)
two 400g (14oz) cans of chopped tomatoes	45ml (3 level tbsp) chopped fresh parsley
300ml (½ pint) dry red wine	

1 Heat the oil in a large, heavy-based saucepan, add the celery, carrots, onion, mushrooms and garlic, and fry for about 5 minutes or until softened. Add the tomato purée and fry for 1 minute, then add all the remaining ingredients, except the parsley. Bring to the boil, then reduce the heat, cover and simmer gently for 30–45 minutes or until the TVP is very tender.

2 Stir in the parsley and season with more salt, pepper and nutmeg, if necessary. Remove the cinnamon stick, bay leaf and bouquet garni before serving.

Vegetable stock

If using onion skins, remove them after 30 minutes or the stock will be bitter.

Makes about 1.1 litres (2 pints)

30ml (2 tbsp) vegetable oil	vegetable trimmings, such as celery tops, cabbage leaves, Brussels sprout leaves, mushroom peelings, tomato skins and potato peelings
1 onion, skinned and finely chopped	
1 carrot, washed and diced	
50g (2oz) turnip, washed and diced	onion skins (optional)
50g (2oz) parsnip, washed and diced	bouquet garni
4 celery sticks, washed and roughly chopped	6 whole black peppercorns

1 Heat the oil in a large saucepan, add the onion and fry gently for about 5 minutes or until soft and lightly coloured.

2 Add the other vegetables to the pan with any vegetable trimmings, outer leaves or peelings available. If a dark brown coloured stock is required, add onion skins.

3 Cover the vegetables with 1.7 litres (3 pints) cold water and add the bouquet garni and peppercorns. Bring to the boil.

4 Half cover the pan and simmer the stock for 1½ hours, skimming occasionally with a slotted spoon.

5 Strain the stock into a bowl and leave to cool. Cover and chill in the refrigerator. This stock will only keep for 1–2 days, after which time it will begin to go sour.

Gravy

It's not difficult to make a delicious vegetarian gravy, providing you use a good, well flavoured stock. Add a dash or two of gravy browning or yeast extract to get a dark brown colour, if necessary.

Makes about 450ml (¾ pint)

15ml (1 tbsp) vegetable oil	30ml (2 level tbsp) plain white flour
1 large onion, skinned and chopped	
125g (4oz) mushrooms, wiped and chopped	600ml (1 pint) vegetable stock
1 garlic clove, skinned and crushed (optional)	a sprig of fresh thyme
	salt and pepper

1 Heat the oil in a heavy-based saucepan. Add the onion, mushrooms and garlic, if using. Fry over a high heat for about 10 minutes or until the onions start to turn golden brown. Stir all the time so that they brown evenly rather than burn.

2 Add the flour and cook over a low heat for about 5 minutes or until the flour starts to brown, stirring all the time. Take the pan off the heat and leave to cool for 1–2 minutes.

3 Gradually blend in the stock, return to the heat and bring to the boil. Add the thyme, season with salt and pepper, lower the heat, cover and simmer for 20 minutes. Strain into a clean saucepan. Taste and adjust the seasoning, if necessary, and reheat just before serving.

Speedy tomato sauce for pasta

My son adores pasta with tomato sauce, but like most young children, once he's decided that he's hungry, he wants to eat immediately. Hence this speedy pasta sauce.
If using dried pasta, look out for quick-cooking 'angel hair' pasta (it's like very fine spaghetti) or small pasta shapes. If you're using larger shapes, put the water on to boil when you start making the sauce. Better still, use quicker-cooking fresh pasta.

Serves 2

15ml (1 tbsp) olive oil	30ml (2 tbsp) tomato purée
1 carrot, peeled and coarsely grated	5ml (1 tsp) sugar
1 large courgette, trimmed and coarsely grated	a handful of fresh basil, chopped, or 5ml (1 level tsp) dried marjoram or oregano
1 garlic clove, skinned and crushed	salt and pepper
400g (14oz) can of chopped tomatoes	grated Parmesan or vegetarian Cheddar cheese, to serve

1 Heat the oil in a large saucepan and sauté the carrot and courgette for 2 minutes or until softened. Add the garlic, tomatoes, tomato purée, sugar and herbs. Season with salt and pepper and bring to the boil, then lower the heat and simmer for about 10 minutes, stirring occasionally.

2 Pour over hot, freshly cooked pasta, top with grated cheese and serve immediately.

NUTRITION

Good source of

VA   VC

Tomato sauce for pasta

This sauce takes longer to cook and is a little more sophisticated than the Speedy tomato sauce given on page 125. Don't throw away leftovers – toss sauce and pasta together and refrigerate until the next day, then simply reheat, covered with cling film, in the microwave.

Serves 3

30ml (2 tbsp) olive oil	15ml (1 tbsp) tomato purée
1 carrot, peeled and finely chopped	a handful of fresh herbs, such as basil, parsley, oregano or marjoram, chopped, or 5ml (1 level tsp) dried herbs
1 small onion or shallot, skinned and finely chopped	
1 celery stick, finely chopped	150ml (¼ pint) red or white wine, or vegetable stock
1 garlic clove, skinned and crushed	1 bay leaf
400g (14oz) can of chopped tomatoes	salt and pepper

1 Heat the oil in a large, heavy-based saucepan, add the vegetables and garlic, and sauté until softened. Add the remaining ingredients, except salt and pepper, and bring to the boil, then lower the heat and simmer gently for about 30 minutes or until the sauce is reduced and the vegetables are very soft. Remove the bay leaf.

2 If you prefer a smooth sauce, purée the tomato mixture in a blender or food processor. Season with salt and pepper and serve with hot, freshly cooked pasta.

NUTRITION

Good source of

VA VC VE

VARIATIONS

Try these variations with either of the tomato sauce recipes given above.

Roman Sauce Add about 225g (8oz) chopped fresh spinach, a handful of toasted pine nuts (older children only), and a few sultanas or raisins. Heat through to cook the spinach, and season with a little nutmeg.

Tomato and Mascarpone Sauce Add about 45ml (3 tbsp) mascarpone to the finished sauce and heat gently. This makes a deliciously creamy, mild sauce and the mascarpone adds extra protein to the dish.

Spaghetti with Tomato and vegetable sauce

Tomato and Bean Sauce Add 125g (4oz) of your favourite cooked beans or half a 425g (15oz) can of beans, drained and rinsed. I like to add a crushed dried chilli and a handful of chopped fresh coriander, too, but not all children can cope with such strong flavours.

Mushroom and Tomato Sauce Sauté about 125g (4oz) sliced mushrooms with the vegetables.

Tomato and Pesto Sauce This is a good choice if fresh herbs are unavailable and if, like me, you always have a jar of pesto in the refrigerator ready for flavouring sauces and dressings. Simply add about 30ml (2 tbsp) pesto to the finished sauce.

Tomato and Vegetable Sauce Add a handful of frozen peas, 1 courgette, halved lengthways and sliced, or a few halved green beans about 5 minutes before the end of the cooking time.